Create.
an Impression
Landscaping for Curb Appeal

MAGGIE CLAYTON

enjoygardening

23 Complete Designs for Front Yards

HOLE'S

Printed in Canada   5   4   3   2   1

Library and Archives Canada Cataloguing in Publication
Clayton, Maggie, 1949-
    Create an impression : landscaping for curb appeal / Maggie Clayton.

Includes index.
ISBN 978-1-894728-07-6

    1. Landscape gardening. 2. Gardens--Designs and plans. I. Title.

SB473.C63 2006   712'.6   C2006-906401-6

Hole's   Lone Pine Publishing
101 Bellerose Drive   10145-81 Avenue
St. Albert, Alberta, Canada   Edmonton, Alberta
T8N 8N8   T6E 1W9
www.enjoygardening.com

Table of Contents

Dedication

This book is dedicated to the memory of my mother, Lassie Matzen, whose love of gardening and the soil was passed to me through her example...and maybe even her DNA.

Foreword

Have you ever wondered why we prefer one type of land-scape over another? The obvious answer would seem that it's a matter of personal taste—at least, that's what I thought before I had the opportunity to listen to a lecture that revolved around the con-cept of biophilia, which, in a nutshell, is the innate affiliation people seek with the natural world. The lecturer suggested that humans have specific landscape preferences that are based on thousands of years of evolution. Those preferences are for landscapes that offer access to sources of food and water, shelter and vantage points that allow us to see but not be seen by sharp-toothed predators.

Perhaps it's because I really don't want it to be true, but I'm not con-vinced that I plant trees because of some Darwinian desire to hide from enemies. However, there is no denying that people spend lots of time and money trying to create the perfect yard.

Everyone seems to have a different idea of what perfection is, but chances are, if you have a nicely landscaped front yard, you probably know it—and not because of ego but because of the parade of vehicles and foot traffic that slows down as it passes your home. You can also be sure that many of those passersby have tried to recreate what they've seen. Unfor-tunately, many people don't realize that beautiful front yards are patiently planned and carefully executed—often in stages. At our greenhouse, we see a lot of frustrated people who have spent the summer removing cedars that have grown into the eaves and spruce trees that cover windows. The frustrating part for us is to see customers rushing to replace these plants, seemingly determined to trade one mistake for another. Everyone makes mistakes, but coming up with a thought out plan will increase your chance of ending up with a front yard you can enjoy.

So let thousands of years of evolu-tion guide you, if you must, but then seek out the best sources of informa-tion you can find and design a land-scape that will give you the front yard you've always wanted.

–Jim Hole
Hole's Greenhouses and Gardens

Preface

From Experience, Grows Expertise

I've heard a lot of knowledgable people, on a lot of different subjects, say they never thought they'd write a book, so I consider myself in good company. Although I've been offering my advice and design services for years, it hadn't occurred to me to bind that knowledge between two covers. That changed when Hole's Publishing asked if I was interested in taking on that task. They thought a book of landscape designs for front yards would be helpful both to novice gardeners and to the more experienced who wanted to give their landscapes some extra appeal. What they described was the exact book I wished was available, so I agreed.

The second reason I agreed to write this book is because I have made nearly every gardening mistake there is. Having learned from every one, I hope to share my knowledge and save others from making similar mistakes. The result is the book you now hold.

Create an Impression—Landscaping for Curb Appeal provides examples of front yards, each with its own set of issues, and explains and illustrates how I have chosen to address each situation. I must stress that every garden in this book is unique and that the choices I have made for each design may not apply to every reader's situation or desire—there is no such thing as the "right" design. Two designers will likely come up with two different ideas for any given situation, or one designer will come up with several—all equally valid. However, I hope that what is contained in these pages will inspire people to consider different options that will allow them to not only design a front yard, but also to create an impression.

–Maggie Clayton

Introduction

Maggie Clayton has a Bachelor of Arts degree as well as a diploma in
Landscape Architectural Technology. In the 10 years she's worked at Hole's
Greenhouses and Gardens, she's helped gardeners of all levels select the right
plants for the right locations. In doing so, she's gained invaluable knowledge
about the trees, shrubs and perennials that grow in our climate and a
tremendous respect for the heart and hard work that go into gardening.

I am a lazy gardener. To me, a garden is something to enjoy. A place to sit, relax and savour a cup of coffee on a quiet Sunday morning. A place to admire the way the light plays between a 'Silver & Gold' dogwood and a 'Tannenbaum' pine. What it should not be is a place to think about the hour or two you'll need to find to cut back that dogwood because it was planted too close to the house in a 1m wide bed. But that's not to say that my garden takes care of itself. There are always times of concerted effort in the spring and the fall when I am planting something, but because I've planned my garden carefully, the rest of the time is often of benign neglect. I will water, weed or prune when necessary but won't spend hours fussing and tweaking.

Not only am I lazy, but I am also cheap. On my daily walks around the neighbourhood with our dog, Sam, I see many beds expensively mulched with designer rock. The freshly landscaped ones we come across always look lovely, but as we walk through the older parts of the subdivision and see once-new, lava stone beds filled with thistles, dandelions and an assortment of other weeds, I can't help but cringe at thought of the maintenance involved in keeping a new bed looking new. Weeds are hard enough to remove from bare soil—just think about trying to pull them after they've set roots into landscape fabric. Using a herbicide called glyphosate will help, but applying it involves either carefully protecting the plants you want to keep or painstakingly painting the herbicide onto the weeds—it sounds too much like work for me. Besides, wasn't that landscape fabric and rock supposed

to stop weeds in the first place? Sorry. Nothing will. No, if I am going to spend a significant amount of money on a landscaping element, it will be on something that has lasting value. Also, given the choice, I prefer to buy most plants in their smaller, more economical sizes and wait the few years it takes them to mature. Besides providing me with the pleasure of watching my garden grow, starting with small plants also appeals to my laziness: the plants require a smaller hole and, therefore, less planting effort. Within three to five years, the garden will look as mature as one planted with larger materials.

Our little plots of land must not only complement the homes that sit on them, they must also complement their surrounding neighbourhoods. That's why having a broad view of landscaping, one that takes the whole street into consideration, is best.

If You Don't Have a Plan, You Don't Have a Clue

In order to have a successful garden, you need to have an idea of what you have and what you want, but—most importantly—you need to have a plan from which to work. You can come up with that plan yourself or hire a professional designer to help; just make sure you are making informed decisions that are right for you. Unfortunately, bad advice is often disguised as best intentions, and in gardening, as in life, best intentions have a way of going something like this...

A new bride was in the kitchen preparing her first turkey dinner. Her adoring and liberated husband was giving a helping hand when he saw her cut the parson's nose off the turkey. He lovingly enquired as to the reason for its removal, and she sweetly replied that it was how her mother always did it. Being a rational man and also a brave one, he called his mother-in-law to find out why that step was necessary. She told him that it was just the proper way to do it because it was how her mother always prepared the turkey. Persisting in his enquiry, he called Grandma and asked her the same question. She replied that that cutting off the parson's nose was the only way she could get the turkey to fit into her pan.

Unfortunately, that is how we often approach landscaping our gardens. We simply do what everyone else has done—regardless of whether or not it has merit or applies to our situation.

Common Landscape Mistakes

Mistakes are easy to make. Unfortunately, some of the most common landscaping errors are inspired by guiding resources that fail us—magazines that show lovely, but questionably planted, trees and shrubs in gardens that have been carefully groomed for photo shoots come to mind. Although the glossy pictures are inspiring, what they don't show are the homeowners digging out their mistakes a few years later. To avoid hard lessons, keep the following common mistakes in mind:

- We plant too close to our houses, sidewalks, driveways, fences and property lines.
- We choose the wrong plant.
- We don't prepare the soil properly.
- We don't account for wind or stagnant air.
- We plant without considering the mature height and spread of a tree.
- We don't give the plants a good growing environment.

A customer brought a dead lilac in to the nursery, wondering why it died. One sniff at the roots and the cause was obvious: rot. I asked where it was planted, and the customer said that it was next to the downspout. This is a case of not considering the growing environment when selecting a plant. A dogwood or a willow would have been a better choice for a wet area.

It seems hard to believe that the tiny shrub we bring home from the garden centre will ever grow to the size noted on the plant tag—but it will, and often beyond the places we want it to.

Wondering About Watering?

The only watering rule most gardeners are taught is to water plants thoroughly enough to get them established. Hmm…perhaps that seems like a bit of a cop-out, but because water requirements are subject to so many variables, it's almost impossible to be more specific.

How much water a plant needs is dependant on many factors:

- It depends on sun exposure. A plant in a sunny, hot spot will need to be watered more frequently than one in the shade.
- It depends on soil composition. Soil that is clay based will retain more water than sandy soil will.
- It depends on the weather. If it is hot, you may need to water every other day to establish your plants. If it is hot and windy, you may need to water every day. If it's cool—maybe every three or four days.
- It might depend on the potting media. Many drought-tolerant plants seem to be potted in a very porous medium, perhaps to keep their roots from rotting. Unfortunately, this medium dries out quickly and these plants might require more frequent watering.
- It depends on you. If you lay down landscape fabric and rock mulch soon after planting (not recommended by the nursery trade), the soil may not have dried out at all and the plants may not need to be watered in.
- It depends on the plant itself. Some plants need to stay consistently moist, while others will fare better if the surface of the soil dries out between waterings.

Foundation Plantings: Why we have it all wrong

A foundation planting is a bed of plants located next to the foundation of a building, and its purpose is to marry the building to its surroundings. In and of itself, there is nothing wrong with a conventional foundation planting, especially if it hides a mass of unattractive parging; however, many houses today have attractive brick or stone finishes that are a shame to cover. It can be hard to break from convention, but just because we've approached foundation planting a certain way in the past, doesn't mean it's the best way to do it.

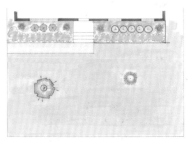

Illustration A

Illustration B

Typically, people take a similar approach to landscaping. They move into a new home and get everything in order indoors before thinking about the outside. When the time to landscape does come, homeowners often step outside their front door, look at where the bottom step of their front landing ends and start their foundation bed there. The more industrious might go to the trouble of building a raised bed. The next step is usually a trip to the nearest garden centre, where the homeowner will pick out a tree or two and a selection of shrubs that strike their fancy. All that's left to do is to take them home and bung them in the ground. Done. Easy peasy.

Unfortunately, that approach to landscaping is not an exaggeration. The result is usually a bed that is too close to the house, sometimes projecting only as far as the roof overhang. In this environment, the plants are often starved for space, light or water. More often than not, the trees and shrubs quickly outgrow their space, cover the windows and crowd the front door.

For arguments sake, I have drawn an example of a typical foundation planting (see Illustrations A and B). It depicts a bed planted and spaced in an attractive manner. Not a lot of thought has gone into the design, but it looks fine.

Now let's project into the future (see Illustration C).

The shade tree has blotted out the front window, the spruce has overtaken one side of the yard and the cedars, which are preparing to grow into the eaves, are also beginning to encroach on the front door. The house is hidden behind the plants, and it looks like the only way to get to the front door is by cutting across the lawn.

For some reason, even though we see these problems all the time, we continue to plant the same way, forgetting that the purpose of a front garden is to anchor a home within the landscape—not to have the landscape overtake the home.

Even a well-planned foundation bed may not give a homeowner value for his or her money. Why? Often, the design is such that it can be appreciated only from the street, which means the only time the homeowners can enjoy their garden is on the way home from work or when they are coming back from walking the dog. Wouldn't it be preferable to sit in one's living room and look onto a mixed bed of shrubs and flowers than at the garage across the street? Another problem with traditional front gardens is that they aren't used. The only time owners seem to be out front is when they are working on the yard: cutting the lawn, deadheading the flowers, etc. Other than using the step to rest on, they have little opportunity to enjoy the space. A better design would incorporate an area where homeowners could sit with a neighbour, enjoy a glass of iced tea and, literally, take time to smell the roses.

Illustration C

Now let's take the same house I showed all the mistakes on and look at what happens when the landscaping is given a bit of thought (see Illustrations D and E). Here, only a few more plants have been used, but they have been spaced according to their mature sizes. Some curved beds have been added beyond the foundation, and a generous path to the front door has been installed. The yard looks a little sparse initially, but that can be resolved by strategically placing a few pots of annuals in empty spaces.

Now, let's project ourselves into the future again (see illustration F). The house looks cozy—not crowded—and

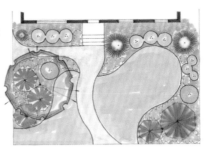

Illustration D

we can still see it! Because the beds were designed to be enjoyed from more than one vantage point, the homeowners have an interesting view from their living room, as well as from the street.

Illustration E

Illustration F

Getting It Right
How to do it properly and why

It really takes only a bit of planning and inspiration to create an interesting yard that can be enjoyed. Unfortunately, the sameness of our suburbs is often compounded by the sameness of the landscapes growing within them. How can we remedy this? We can begin by thinking of our front yards as a kind of personal introduction—an expression of our values, of our style and of ourselves.

In general, we want our homes to look attractive, so any landscaping we do should complement the architecture, scale and colour of our homes. We also want our homes to look welcoming and accessible. This means the route we, as well as our visitors, take from the street to the front door should be well defined, comfortable and pleasant.

From a purely financial standpoint, an attractive front garden will add monetary value to a property.

How are these goals achieved? Start by asking the proper questions.

Must-Ask Questions

If it is at all possible, live in your home through all four seasons *before* you put anything in the ground. Observing your landscape will give you an idea of what environmental conditions you're dealing with and provide you time to ask some important questions:

- What hardiness zone do you live in? Are you located in a brand new subdivision or in an established area? Are there landscaping requirements set by the developer? What are the micro-climates on your property? Where is it baking hot? Where is it wet? What areas get full sun? Where is it shady? Where is it windy? Where is it sheltered? Do you have a drainage pattern that needs to be followed? Are there high-traffic areas in your yard?—this is easy to determine in the winter when you can see footprints in the snow.

The next step is to think about what you wish to achieve in the landscape. Remember, front yards can meet all the needs that backyards can, and sometimes the front yard is the only yard that people have to enjoy.

- Is there a view you want to hide or to accent? How would you like to use a particular area? Do you have young children or plan to start a family? Do you like to entertain? Is there a style of garden you like, and will it complement the architecture of your home? Are there any plants you simply must have or ones you don't like at all?

One way to deal with a tiny front yards is to landscape with a neighbour. This results in a cohesive look and can save money. It's also a great way to build a sense of community.

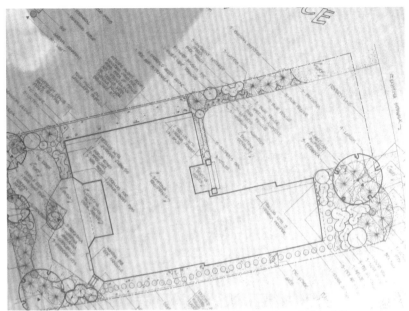

A landscape plan is drawn to scale and includes the location of all buildings and hardscape elements like driveways and sidewalks. It should always acknowledge property lines and right of ways.

Other factors to consider are:

- How long do you anticipate living in your home? What colour is it? How much time are you willing to invest installing and maintaining the landscape? Are you willing to stage the landscape over time, or do you want it done all at once? How much money are you willing to invest? **Note:** It's reasonable to expect to spend 5–10% of the value of your home on landscaping.

Once you have worked through the above questions and are feeling willing and confident, you can begin to design your garden. Using your Surveyor's Certificate or the Real Property Report you received when you purchased your home, you can make a scaled drawing of your property and begin

to work on design ideas. Don't skip this step—it is far easier to rub out a pencil line on a piece of paper than it is to dig up a tree.

But what if you are not willing or don't feel able to come up with a plan? For a moderate cost, you can enlist the help of a landscape designer. In fact, the cost of the design may be more than offset by the potential savings of not needing to redo your garden. If you do choose to go with a designer, make sure you still take the time to go through the above-mentioned list of questions. It will give your designer much of the information he or she will need to create a design with which you will be happy. I must, however, add a note of caution: A landscape design should include where to put a deck/patio, retaining wall, raised bed, sidewalk, etc., so if you are going to use the services of a landscape designer, have the design done *before* you construct or install any of the hardscaping. A beautiful raised bed is of little use if it isn't built to sustain healthy growth of plant material. On several occasions, while working in the nursery at Hole's, I was shown pictures of beautiful retaining walls or raised beds that couldn't support more than a few dwarf plants. The structures were nice, the constuction was perfect, but as far as most plants were concerned, the beds were a travesty.

Another tip I like to give is to start working with your designer in the off-season when things are less hectic. Everything about landscaping comes down to planning, so it is unrealistic to expect a designer or landscape contractor to be readily available if you call them in April or May. Beginning the design process in the fall is a better idea; there is no rush, and it allows you to call contractors in January or February when they are not busy doing installations. I'm giving away my age, but when I was a kid, there were regular ads on the radio and television stating, "Why wait for spring? Do it now!"

Raised beds and terraces may solve grading issues but they need to be wide enough to sustain plant growth.

Soil quality is the single most important factor in plant health. Good soil means good growth.

Soil

Luckily for me, our house was built before land developers got into the habit of stripping away all of the topsoil prior to construction, so when I dig in most areas of my yard, I have to go beyond a spade's depth to hit the clay subsoil. Others are not so fortunate.

Today, many homeowners in newly developed neighbourhoods find themselves faced with a sea of construction-compacted clay and a wealth of potential problems. The rough grade certificate is obtained and, more often than not, barely enough topsoil is brought in to support the growth of a lawn (a minimum 15cm). Small holes are dug into which a tree and a few shrubs are placed. Then, a few years down the road, the question is asked: "Why aren't my plants doing well?" The answer?—improperly prepared soil. To have a planting bed that will sustain plants, the subsoil needs to be removed to sufficient depth to allow for a minimum depth of 30cm of good topsoil—45cm would be better and 60cm would be ideal. A second option is to construct raised beds and to fill them with topsoil.

When we *are* fortunate enough to have good soil, we tend not to respect it. In the fall, we get out our leaf blowers and rakes and remove every fallen leaf we can find so that everything looks neat and tidy. We pull out the annuals, which absorb the soil's nutrients, bag them up and throw them away. It's easy to understand why people want a tidy yard, but without

The optimum depth of a layer of mulch ranges between 5 and 10cm. Clay soils require a thinner layer; sandy soils require a thicker one. Keep mulch away from the bases of all plants to avoid possible problems with rot.

Benefits of using mulch:
- Reduces surface evaporation, which conserves water usage.
- Controls weeds, which compete with plants for soil moisture and nutrients.
- Reduces soil compaction caused by rainfall and foot traffic.
- Keeps roots cool on hot days and warm on cold days.
- Reduces water splash on leaves, which lessens the chance of fungal and bacterial diseases.
- Adds organic matter to the soil as the mulch decomposes.

Drawbacks to using mulch:
- A layer of mulch that's too thick can interfere with air exchange in the root zone.
- Slugs love to hide under mulch.
- Rodents may take up residence in thick mulch.

the added organic matter of decomposing material, our soil gradually loses its structure and fertility. Take a lesson from Mother Nature: leaves and plants are supposed to decompose and return organic material to the soil, which is also the reason why rock mulches aren't a favourite of mine. The rock and its underlying landscape fabric create a barrier that doesn't allow replenishment of the soil. They may also interfere with air exchange at the root zone. This becomes an issue because one quarter of a healthy soil's volume is air.

Sometimes we err on the side of caution, assume the soil we have is bad, remove it and replace it with something like half topsoil and half compost—or worse—potting soil. It might seem like soft soil would provide easy living for a plant, but when the roots of that poor plant eventually

I make compost from the organic waste in my yard and add it to my beds to improve soil quality.

Soil Composition

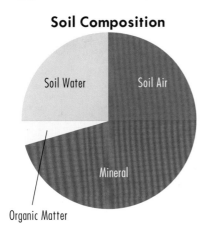

reach the wall of native soil, they are trapped—unable to penetrate beyond the boundary of the hole and wind up growing like a pot-bound houseplant. As indicated by the chart at left, the organic content of loam-type soil is only 5% by volume, so amending soil too much may kill plants with a misplaced kindness. The best thing is either to choose plants that will grow in the soil you have, or to amend the entire bed before you plant, remembering to use only the amount of organic matter that the native soil can handle.

Architecturally Controlled Neighbourhoods

Why do some neighbourhoods have landscaping requirements? It may seem like a strange concept, but a land developer and the municipality to which he or she answers have their own vision of what the neighbourhood should look like. Although they won't dictate what you can plant in your garden, they will require that you put something in it.

If you buy a new home in an architecturally controlled neighbourhood, the developer will give you a list of landscaping requirements and charge you a landscaping security deposit, which will be returned to you when the landscaping is completed—on time and to the minimum standard. Failure to comply

Architecturally controlled neighbourhoods don't have to be boring. Just because plant size is dictated doesn't mean you can't landscape creatively.

Large deciduous trees are most often sold by caliper size.

may mean getting back only part of your deposit or it may be forfeited altogether. Familiarizing yourself with the requirements soon after purchasing your home will allow you time to plan ahead. After all, it's easy enough to make gardening mistakes—no one needs the added pressure of a looming deadline.

Normally, minimum architectural requirements are based on the size of the lot and the type of house. There is also a time limit within which the landscaping must be completed—the sooner grass and trees are planted, the sooner the neighbourhood looks mature and attractive.

The size of the required trees and shrubs are usually specified as follows:

- A deciduous tree is specified by caliper, the diameter of the trunk, measured between 15 and 30cm from the ground.
- A coniferous tree is specified by height, measured from the top of the root ball to the top of the tree.
- Shrubs are specified by height or by spread.

Although finding large shrubs won't be problematic at most garden centres, finding large trees that meet developer's specifications can be tricky. Likely, you will have to purchase them from a local tree nursery where they are grown on site. Top-grafted trees, which are often acceptable for small yards, may also be hard to find.

The Check List: Walk the project through your head and see what you step in

Some gardening programs on television show a landscape project being completed within a couple of days. Expecting yours to be done in that time is unreasonable. It takes planning and time to do a proper job. Even if you have deep pockets and can hire a landscape contractor to manage and execute the work for you, a landscape project takes time.

I've found that the best way to avoid landscaping stumbling blocks is to walk a project through my head before I begin each stage. The following is a check list of 10 steps and reminders that will help you keep your project on track.

Sometimes a landscaping project is just too big to handle on your own. Hiring a professional landscape contractor can save time—and even money—in the long run.

1.

Know where your property line is. This is especially important when it comes to installing a fence. If you and your neighbours choose not to share one, your fence must be within your property—if it encroaches onto your neighbours', they can demand its removal. Also, part of what you think is your lot may belong to the municipality, and permanent structures are likely not allowed in those areas.

2.

For safety's sake, know where your utility lines are. Prior to planting a tree, digging holes for fence posts or footings, removing tree roots, or pounding metal stakes into the ground, you must call your local utility location service and get a locate certificate. These certificates expire, so you many need more than one if you're working in stages.

3.

Check with your municipality to see if you require a building permit.

After completing the first three steps, you can turn your attention to the hardscape elements (patios, walkways, retaining walls) of the design. Since installation of hardscaping may involve the use of heavy equipment, you want to complete this stage before you bring in plant material that may become damaged.

4.

Do the math. If you had a design drawn to scale for you, follow it. If the bed on the drawing is 2m wide, make the actual bed 2m wide. If the path is drawn 1.4m wide, construct it accordingly. Remember, you paid someone for his or her expertise, so don't waste it.

5.

Bring in enough topsoil for the entire project. Even if you are land-scaping in stages, make sure your planting beds are already excavated and have all your topsoil delivered at one time. It will save on costs and spare your yard a second visit from a heavy truck.

6.

Consider installing your lawn at this stage. It's always a good idea to lay your sod before you plant your trees and shrubs. A lawn requires a lot of water to establish itself properly— more water than newly planted trees or shrubs in the area may tolerate.

7.

Plant your trees and shrubs the correct distance from each other and from other elements in the garden (fence, sidewalk, foundation wall, etc.). This will eliminate any problems with crowding and save your plants from having to be dug up and disturbed.

8.

Plant the perennials. Placement of these plants is a bit more flexible because they often need to be lifted and divided after a few years.

9.

Apply organic mulch over the planting area to depth appropriate for your soil type. Clay-based soils need about 5cm of mulch; sandy soils need about 10cm. To avoid the possibility of rot, ensure that the mulch does not cover the trunks, stems or crowns of the plants.

10.

Admire your handiwork and congratulate yourself on a job well done.

Quick Fixes
Short timelines. Small investments.

Not all yard improvements and landscape designs need to be executed in stages over a series of months or summers. Many can be completed in as little as a weekend—but that doesn't mean they don't require thought and planning; they do. So whether you're preparing to spruce up a spruce or to place some statuary, take the time to do it properly—the first time. It will spare you frustrations and save you money.

Staging Your Home for a Quick Sale

The old adage "You get only one chance to make a first impression" is incredibly relevant to selling a home, so before prospective buyers see your property, give some thought as to how it looks from the street. Is it welcoming, colourful and attractive? If you're not satisfied with the answers, there are a few quick things you can do to stage your home.

- Mow, fertilize, water and edge the lawn.
- Weed the planting beds.
- Prune messy shrubs.
- Deadhead perennials and annuals.

- Sweep the entrance and walkway.
- Put away hoses and tools.
- Highlight the front door with a container or two of annuals. If the yard is lacking colour, place additional containers in the planting beds.

Lighting the Yard

Outdoor lights can add interest to your garden and make it safer. Modern architecture and landscapes are particularly dramatic when lit to highlight interesting hardscapes and plantings. Even the shadow a tree casts against a garage wall or a fence can add interest and beauty to a yard. Here are a few lighting methods for you to try:

- Use a floodlight to illuminate or backlight interesting forms, like that of a weeping juniper, a bonsai-pruned Amur maple, an interesting boulder or a piece of statuary.
- Emphasize beautiful bark, like that found on a paper birch or an 'Amur' chokecherry, with an upward beam from an in-ground well light.
- Hang fairy lights (clear Christmas tree lights) on trees or shrubs near patios or decks to create soft lighting for entertaining or to simply provide an enjoyable nighttime view of the garden.
- Illuminate path steps to make them clearly visible.

Placing Boulders

Large rocks or boulders lend interest and a sense of permanence to a landscape. However, before you have large boulders delivered, be absolutely sure of where they are going and to which direction each side should face. I also strongly advise you to be home when they are delivered—if a boulder isn't placed to your liking, you're not likely to be able to change it. Boulders can be selected to blend in with a house or to contrast it, but the main objective is to make them look like they have always been there. It's not as difficult as it might sound, and the following suggestions will help you achieve the look:

- Large boulders always look better when combined with smaller rocks.
- If you are using several boulders, choose similar-looking ones for a unified look—five boulders of differing colours, forms and textures will be visually distracting.
- The bottom third of the rock should be buried to secure it as well as to make it appear established. Just placing a boulder on top of the soil will make it look like you're storing it there until you decide what to do with it.
- You're not going for the Stonehenge look, so don't forget to anchor boulders with plants. Trailing junipers or weeping evergreens look stunning growing around or spilling over stone.

Art in the garden can be functional as well as beautiful. Adding a striking obelisk to an existing bed will create height and interest all year and provide support for plants.

Placing Statuary

I've learned that 'statuary' means many things to many people, but whether it translates to ubiquitous garden gnomes, classical Greek figures or towering inukshuks, using art in the garden is one of the easiest ways to personalize a landscape. Before you place your treasure, consider from which angle you would like to view it. The spot you choose will also need to be level for stability, and in the case of fountains, for proper function. I recommend using a patio block as a base, installed the same way you would a paving stone path. A sturdy, properly installed base will ensure levelness, minimize frost heaving and protect statuary from soil moisture.

The process is quite simple:
- Excavate the area to a depth of about 15cm.
- Put in a 10cm-deep aggregate base (fine gravel), and tamp it down well.
- Spread a 2.5cm layer of sand on top of the aggregate, making sure it is level.
- Place a patio block on top of the sand base, making certain it too is level.
- Set the statuary on the block.

Creating Winter Interest

In my part of the country, much of the garden is dormant for nearly half the year, so it just makes sense to design with winter in mind. Selecting plants that have interesting forms will help create the winter interest your garden may be lacking.

- Many deciduous trees and shrubs, such as burning bush and paper birch, have interesting bark, coloured stems, and/or ornamental fruit that are revealed when their leaves drop.
- Coniferous evergreens add substance to a winter garden and look beautiful dusted with snow and frost.

- A number of herbaceous perennials and annuals, such as grasses and coneflowers, have interesting seed heads, so don't cut them all back during fall cleanup.
- Garden ornaments and furniture look beautiful covered in fresh snow and cast interesting shadow patterns.

Creating Spring Interest

A shot of colour early in the spring is a welcome sight after a long winter.

- Spring flowering bulbs and corms, such as scilla, narcissus, muscari and crocus, provide an early burst of colour. Try interspersing them between later-emerging perennials.
- Many plants bloom before they leaf out: forsythia, some spiraea, double flowering plums and azalea are just a few that brighten the brown landscape of early spring.
- There are a host of perennials (especially alpines) that bloom just as the snow melts. Whitlow grass and pheasant's eye come to mind.

Fixing Up the Yard for a Wedding

Although few weddings are actually held in the front yard, it is the first thing guests see as they arrive. Front yards can also serve as backdrops for photographs. The best advice I can offer is to plan ahead and to let the season of the event be your guide.

Spring weddings:

Pots of flowering spring bulbs are great for adding bursts of colour and elegance to a yard. It takes a bit of time to prepare them in the fall, but they are well worth the effort.

- In the fall, plant up containers with spring flowering bulbs.
- Bury the entire container in the garden and leave it there until spring—if you are using a decorative pot, wrap it in burlap to help keep it clean.
- Dig up the pot as soon as the ground thaws.
- Place the pot in a suitable location and wait for the blooms.

Summer weddings:

- Local garden centres have a wide variety of pre-planted containers and hanging baskets that are perfect for adding colour and style to a front yard. If it's height you're interested in or have a lot of empty space to fill, you might want to enquire about renting some tall potted cedars from a garden centre.
- Dress up the entrance to the house with pots of tender roses. Buy them pre-potted (not bare root) as soon as they are available in the spring and then transplant them into decorative containers.

Fall weddings:

- Plant up containers for your summer enjoyment, but include some plants, such as ornamental grasses and rudbeckia, that hold their interest well into the fall. Any of the annuals that don't survive cooler fall temperatures may be replaced with cold-tolerant pansies.
- Fall mums come in a huge array of colours and, when placed in containers, will brighten any entrance.

Winter weddings:

- Use the pruned branches of dogwoods or junipers in containers along with some purchased pine or spruce boughs to create arrangements for your entrance, window boxes and wall planters.
- Decorative lights can look particularly beautiful during the dark months of winter. A couple of shrubs decked out with mini lights by the entrance will be a sufficient welcome.
- Make ice votives to place strategically around the garden. Fill them with mountain ash berries or leaves saved from the fall.

Proper Pruning Techniques

When clients ask me for low-maintenance plants, I remind them that low maintenance does not mean *no* maintenance. To keep plants—even low maintenance ones—looking their best, you need to prune them regularly.

Proper pruning involves two different techniques, and most shrubs require both methods. Using only one method will result in an unnatural looking and, potentially, diseased plant.

1. **Heading back:** reducing the length of the branch by cutting it back to an outward facing bud or to a good lateral branch.
2. **Thinning:** removing an entire branch, either to a main branch or to the ground.

Potentillas are prime examples of shrubs that benefit from heading back one year and thinning the next to produce a full, healthy form.

Candle pruning a pine.

Pruning a Coniferous Shrub

When I use the term coniferous shrub, I'm referring to those wonderful smaller versions of needle and cone-bearing plants, such as fir, pine, spruce and larch.

Plants are pruned to maintain form, to direct growth, to contain size and to remove dead, damaged or diseased material. Prune coniferous shrubs early in the summer while they are actively growing. The technique you use will be determined by the species of the plant. Because conifers grow only from the tips, renewal pruning (thinning) is not an option. Therefore, if the conifer becomes overgrown, it will likely require removal. To keep a coniferous shrub looking its best, begin a pruning regimen early in its life.

- Pines are 'candle' pruned. This is done by cutting back the new growth by up to a third just as the new needles are beginning to emerge.
- The new growth on spruce may be cut back by up to a third, but do this when the needles have emerged and the stem is still soft.
- The new, soft growth on cedars and upright junipers may be sheared back by up to a third.
- Spreading junipers may be cut back to the first fork in the branches (or more) if required. Do not shear.

General notes of caution when pruning

A good pruning job is one that makes the tree or shrub look better—but still natural. Take the following information into consideration before you begin pruning:

- If you do not have a valid reason to prune, don't.
- If the branches are high and require a ladder to reach, call in a certified arborist. Safety should always come first.
- If your tree or shrub has gotten out of control, remember that it took a few years for it to get that way and that it will take a few years to get it back into shape. Many trees and shrubs have been mutilated by some one who thinks he or she can fix the problem in one afternoon.

Rejuvenating a Deciduous Hedge

Despite our best intentions, sometimes a hedge can get out of our control, and in the case of cotoneaster hedges, may become infested with scale insects or become susceptible to fire blight. Instead of ripping out the hedge, why not consider reviving it by following this method:

Note: Before attempting this process, make sure the shrubs with which you are dealing can withstand this drastic pruning method: caragana, honeysuckle and alpine currant are a few of the toughest in my area.

- Use sharp-bladed, long-handled lopping shears to cut back the plants to just above ground level. The best time to do this is in late winter or early spring, before bud break. Do not use a chain saw for this step—it will create ragged cuts and be dangerous to use at this angle. The loppers will make clean cuts that will help prevent fungal or bacterial disease from entering the plant. If you are rejuvenating a fire blight-stricken hedge, you will need to disinfect your blade with a 10% solution of bleach and water after each cut.

- Water and fertilize the hedge while it reestablishes. Drought will only stress it out.

- Keep to a regular pruning schedule once the shrubs begin to grow back.

Sprucing Up a Spruce

Well-established evergreen trees often take on a shabby-looking appearance due to a buildup of dead twigs and branches within their centres, but take heart—cleaning up deadwood is a good way to build up your confidence about pruning! Here's how I clean up my trees:

Note: You will need a sharp pair of secateurs, a sharp pruning saw, safety glasses and long sleeves to protect your arms. A sturdy ladder is also helpful.

- Work your way into the centre of the tree and begin to examine the branches, starting with the bottom ones.

- If a branch is completely dead, clip or saw it off at the branch collar, being careful not to leave any stubs. **Note:** Do not make a flush cut into the bark of the trunk—it will lead to rot and disease.
- Green growth at the tip of a branch means the branch is alive. Clean up these branches by clipping off all of the dead twigs and branchlets that have no green growth on them.
- Gradually work your way up the tree, as high as your comfort level will let you.

Putting Up the Right Fence

Front yards in subdivisions are often left unfenced, and in some ways, that's a pity. The right fence can frame a landscape beautifully and provide a great backdrop for plants. Fences can also make us feel less exposed and more at ease about spending time in the front yard. Here are a few things to consider about fences:

- The fence you choose should complement the style of your home. An ultra-modern home, for example, would look bizarre surrounded by a white picket fence.
- The fence should also be in keeping with the particular style, if any, of your garden. A metal chain link fence is an economical, low maintenance fence, but it would look out of place in an English garden.
- There are lots of material choices for constructing a fence: wood, wrought iron and PVC-composites are all options.
- The finish on the fence can also be chosen to complement your home. Some materials, like cedar, look very attractive in their natural state.

If you are waiting for plants to grow at the base of a fence and want a quick way to break up the long expanse, try mounting sturdy, attractive hooks on the posts and hang baskets overflowing with colourful trailing annuals.

Container Gardening

Container gardening is a trend that's enjoying a surge of popularity. Perhaps it's because we lead busy lives and find containers easier to maintain than large landscapes, or maybe it's because we have less space and the appropriately sized container fits the bill beautifully. Whatever the reason, containers can be placed anywhere plants can't grow—and anywhere they can. Try them along driveways, on either side of garage doors, along the edge of sidewalks, hanging from arbours, fences or eaves, mounted under windows or on walls. You can even place them in planting beds for a shot of added height and colour. Here are some things to consider when selecting and maintaining containers:

The container:

- Choose a container that fits its function: hanging baskets can't be so large as to be ridiculously heavy when watered, and pots must be large enough to accommodate a showy amount of plants and enough soil to sustain them.
- All containers must have drainage holes to allow excess water to drain away.
- A container should be in scale with its location. Nothing looks sillier than two, tiny faux-cast iron urns flanking an imposing double garage door.

Soil:

- It is best to use a soil-less mix, either peat based or compost based. This type of planting medium has a light texture and allows for proper aeration. Top soil compacts and should never be used.
- If the container is really big and you don't want to fill the entire pot with soil, place a filler material, such as Styrofoam packing peanuts or empty pop cans, in the bottom of the pot and then add the planting medium. This works well if you are planting annuals in a vessel that is particularly deep. Just be sure to always have at least 35 to 45cm of planting medium in the container.

Watering:

- After planting your container, water it thoroughly—water should begin to drain out the bottom of the pot. This will ensure that the entire root zone is properly moistened.
- Check the containers daily and water thoroughly as required, ensuring that the entire root zone is irrigated.

Fertilizing:

- Nutrients in the planting medium are leached away with every watering, so you will need to fertilize the containers on a regular basis (once a week) with a water-soluble fertilizer. If you choose to fertilize at every watering, just add a pinch to the watering can.

- If you don't like using water-soluble fertilizer, you can purchase a slow-release fertilizer to sprinkle on or in the planting medium.

Plant material:

- Virtually anything may be planted in a container; the only catch is that small trees, shrubs and herbaceous perennials may perish in them over the winter. If you want to keep these plants from season to season, you will have to either bury the entire container in the ground in the fall or remove and transplant the plants into the garden in the fall.
- Ornamental grasses look fantastic in containers and create winter interest.
- Tender roses are quite attractive planted in containers.
- Using a variety of materials will add dimension to your container: try trailing plants that spill over the edges, plants with interesting texture and blooms and plants that add height.

Adding Colour

Spinning the colour wheel

When customers ask for advice about purchasing trees or shrubs, I often ask what colour their house is. Why? Plants placed close to the house should stand out—otherwise, why bother? Keep the following considerations in mind if you want to punch up your yard with colour:

- Variegated plants will just fade away if planted next to light-coloured walls. A plant with dark-green leaves would look much better.
- Shrubs with yellow foliage look great planted next to a blue house and create a complementary colour combination.
- Purple-foliaged plants stand out nicely against pinkish stucco homes and create an analogous colour scheme.
- Contrast and balance are important elements in the garden. If everything is the same value of colour, the garden will look flat. If everything is of a different value, it will look too busy. What looks best is a balanced colour combination— this means combining a grouping of similar coloured plants with a single contrasting plant (a focal point). This can be achieved by simply planting a variegated plant among a group of solid-coloured plants.

The barberry in front of this home is not only poorly placed but its rich colour is also lost in a background of red brick.

The Designs

Ibelieve that gardening should be a pleasure and that there is an ideal landscape design for every gardener—regardless of his or her level of experience or the location of his or her land. As I've previously mentioned, a plan can make the difference between having a nice landscape and having a spectacular one—one that welcomes visitors and says my home belongs here. A solid landscape plan or design can help your property become not only appealing, but also a truly useful and smart extension of your home.

To that end, the designs presented in this section have been created in easy-to-execute steps, using commonly available plants. This format allows gardeners to approach their landscape projects in stages according to time, budget and desire. The plant selections, however, are not set in stone. In fact, if you can't find a suggested plant, please refer to "The Plants" section (beginning on page 184) for more details on the plants, their uses and suggested substitutions. Whether you are landscaping a new property or hoping to revive and polish a tired one, there is sure to be a plan here to meet your needs.

You may notice in my designs that there is often nothing planted closer than 1m from the house foundations. I consider this to be a "dead zone" because it is a difficult area in which to grow anything—so why bother at all? Also, the only time you will notice that there isn't anything planted there is if you are standing close to the house. Instead, I encourage you to mulch any bare ground. Besides looking nice, it prevents soil from washing away or splashing onto foliage or the walls, and through the magic of visual foreshortening, the empty space will be unnoticeable from a distance.

You may also notice that I have used either straight lines or large curves to create the planting beds. To me, they are better defined and more pleasing to the eye. A lot of squiggly curves are not only distracting, but also murder to mow around.

How to Read the Landscape Plans

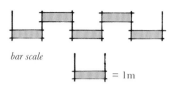

Before you begin, there are a few
things you need to know about how
to read and use the landscape designs.

bar scale

$\vdash\hspace{-0.5em}\dashv$ = 1m

- The plans have been drawn to a
  1:100 scale and each has a bar scale from which to work.
- Each bar on the bar scale represents 1m. In the process of this book's produc-
  tion, the plan views may have been either reduced or enlarged, so to use the
  scale, simply line up a piece of paper to the scale, mark off each unit onto the
  paper and this will give you a ruler with which to measure the plan.

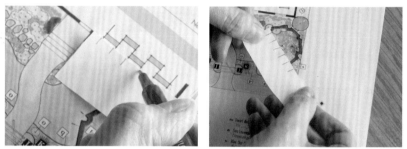

*To use the scale on the landscape plans, line up a piece of paper to the scale, mark
off the units on the paper and use the paper as a ruler with which to measure the
plans.*

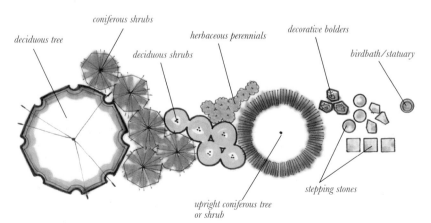

*Reading a landscape design plan is really just a matter of familiarizing yourself
with some of the basic shapes used to depict elements.*

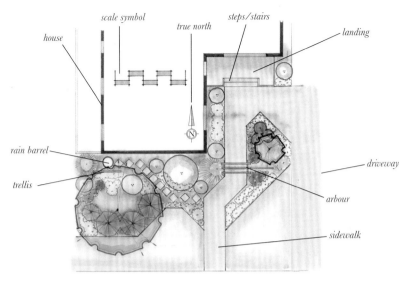

scale symbol — *true north* — *steps/stairs* — *landing* — *house* — *rain barrel* — *trellis* — *arbour* — *driveway* — *sidewalk*

Designs reproduced in a small format can be difficult to interpret. Read the accompanying text for each plan to gain a thorough understanding.

- Each plan has accompanying text that explains the decisions made in regard to each landscape. This will help you decide if a particular plan suits your front yard.
- The elevations (the face-on views of the landscapes) are my visions for what I hope to achieve in each design. The graphics in the elevations show the general form of the plants but are not true representations of any particular plant. Sadly, I am not an artist.
- Trees, shrubs and roses are represented on the plans by uppercase letters in black boxes; perennials by lowercase in white boxes.
- The quantity of plants required in a single grouping is listed in brackets following the plant's Latin name. For example, if you see (3) + (3) next to a plant name, it indicates that there are two different groupings of three plants in the design.

A completed elevation.

A Cottage Garden

Insufficient access to front door,
colonial-style house, southern exposure

Wish List: roses, cottage-style garden and defined borders.

*A couple and their teenaged children have recently relocated
and are interested in landscaping their new front yard. Now
that their children are older, the parents have more time to
dedicate to gardening. They are avid do-it-yourselfers, and
the husband enjoys woodworking. Both have expressed an
interest in growing roses in an informal garden and aren't
concerned with the amount of maintenance required. They
understand the work involved in creating a cottage-style
garden and would like to install theirs in manageable stages.*

Stage Three elevation

The Plan

Assessing the Design Options

The homeowners are interested in creating a cottage-style garden—a style that is similar but slightly more structured than an English garden—to complement the colonial look of their home. Bringing in a quantity of good soil will be a vital step in creating the full beds they envision. They'd also like to install a wide, gently curved path that leads to the front door from the street, as well as a second path that leads from the front door to the driveway. The addition of an open-work lattice fence and a matching trellis will define the yard's borders while still maintaining an open airy feel.

Landscape Tip

If you want to create a sheltered area by putting up a fence, keep in mind that a solid fence might not accomplish the task. In fact, it's likely to create turbulence on the leeward side. An open-style fence is a better option because it will dissipate the wind.

A Cottage Garden—Stage One

This stage of the design begins with the installation of a trellis next to the front steps. It will be made of open-work lattice, the same material from which the fence will be constructed. A 1.5m wide, gently curved concrete path that starts at the street and ends at the steps of the front door will also be added. The second, narrower path that leads from the front entrance to the driveway will be replaced with one made of flagstones.

Next, a large bed will be created to span the entire front of the house. The concrete path and front steps will divide this foundation bed in half. Planting a 'Fuchsia Girl' crabapple on the western half of the bed and a 'Summerwine' ninebark on the eastern side will create a strong contrast against the light-coloured clapboard siding of the house. The 'Morden Centennial' and 'Morden Sunrise' roses are hardy varieties that overwinter without requiring protection. The roses I've suggested may be substituted with English roses if the homeowners feel adventurous and want to push the zones—but they'll have to provide winter protection. The west bed features a 'Bailey Compact' cranberry to provide spring and fall interest and 'Annabelle' hydrangeas to act as a strong late summer feature. A 'Taunton's Spreading' yew is my nod to an English-type of evergreen and should do well in this location, but if the homeowners are nervous about hardiness, a nest spruce could be substituted.

On the western side of the front entrance, 'Polish Spirit' clematis will be grown on the new trellis, and the rest of the perennials I've chosen are also typically identified with an English garden. Thyme will be planted along the flagstone path to emphasize the desired informal cottage style.

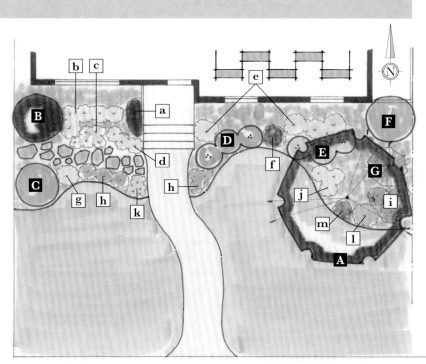

Trees

A Ornamental Crabapple 'Fuchsia Girl'
Malus..(1)

Shrubs

B Ninebark 'Summer Wine'
Physocarpus opulifolius
'Seward'.......................................(1)

C Rose 'Morden Centennial'
Rosa...(1)

D Rose 'Morden Sunrise'
Rosa...(3)

E Hydrangea 'Annabelle'
Hydrangea arborescens.............(3)

F Cranberry 'Bailey Compact'
Viburnum trilobum.....................(1)

G Yew 'Taunton's Spreading'
Taxus x media 'Tauntonii'...........(1)

Perennials

a Virgin's Bower Clematis 'Polish Spirit'
Clematis viticella......................(1)

b Obedient Plant
Physostegia virginiana.............(5)

c Maiden Pink
Dianthus deltoides..................(5)

d Blue Fescue *Festuca glauca*........(3)

e Delphinium *Delphinium*.....(1) + (3)

f Peony *Paeonia*............................(1)

g Daylily *Hemerocallis*..................(1)

h Coralbells *Heuchera*..........(3) + (3)

i Blue Sage 'May Night'
Salvia x sylvestris....................(3)

j Threadleaf Tickseed 'Zagreb'
Coreopsis verticillata...............(3)

k Creeping Speedwell
Veronica oltensis......................(3)

l Hosta 'Francee' *Hosta*.................(1)

m Dwarf Bearded Iris 'Boo'
Iris ....(1)

The Cottage Garden—Stage Two

Stage Two of this design calls for the installation of an open-lattice fence with an arbour over a gate. It also focuses on extending the planting beds around the entire perimeter of the front yard, within the fence's boundaries. Extending the beds will leave a kidney-shaped lawn in the middle of the yard (divided roughly in half by the concrete path).

The arbour I've selected has a gable-style top that matches the pitch of the home's roof. Its peak will be an excellent place to put the house number. Although the arbour is designed to be wide enough to allow clear passage, the 'John Davis' rose I've chosen to grow on it has fewer thorns than most roses, which makes it a good choice for this high foot traffic area. A fragrant 'Blanc Double de Coubert' rose will repeat the bloom colour of both the hydrangeas and the cranberry planted in Stage One.

The addition of two upright junipers planted on the west side of the bed will create a strong vertical element. More perennials added at this stage will provide seasonal interest: lilies interplanted with narcissus will provide both spring and summer interest, and during the late part of the summer, Sweet Joe Pye will add its fragrance to that of the neighbouring Blanc Double de Coubert rose.

The addition of the lattice fence, at this stage in the design, will give the garden a strong sense of separation from the street yet allow the plants to be viewed by passersby.

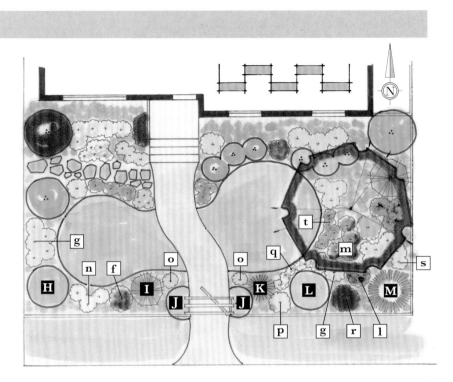

Shrubs

H Lilac 'Miss Kim'
   Syringa patula ....(1)

I Spruce 'Pumila' *Picea abies* ....(1)

J Rose 'John Davis'
   Rosa ....(2)

K Juniper 'Blue Arrow'
   Juniperus scopulorum ....(1)

L Rose 'Blanc Double
   de Coubert' *Rosa* ....(1)

M Juniper 'Idyllwild'
   Juniperus virginiana ....(1)

Perennials

f Peony *Paeonia*............................(1)

g Daylily *Hemerocallis*.........(5) + (1)

l Blue Sage 'May Night'
   Salvia x *sylvestris* ....(1)

m Dwarf Bearded Iris 'Boo'
   Iris .... (3)

n Sea Lavender
   Limonium platyphyllum..............(3)

o Blue Oat Grass
   Helictotrichon sempervirens....(2)

p False Sunflower 'Summer Sun'
   Heliopsis helianthoides
   var. *scabra*..................................(1)

q Cottage Pinks
   Dianthus plumarius..................(7)

r Sweet Joe Pye
   Eupatorium purpureum..............(1)

s Lily Pixie Series *Lilium* .... (7)
   interplant with Daffodil (Narcissus)
   for spring colour

t Greyleaf Cranesbill 'Ballerina'
   Geranium cinereum..................(5)

The Cottage Garden—Stage Three

This final stage of creating this cottage-style garden is aimed at marrying the lot to its most public edge. Another bed is to be installed on the outside perimeter between the fence and the public sidewalk.

A low hedge of 'Russian Globe' caragana planted nearest the sidewalk will enclose the other plants in this bed but not hide them. These caraganas are hardy and drought tolerant, but if the owners prefer, they can opt for a variety of boxwood deemed hardy for their area—although I find the caragana more reliable. With the exception of a 'Dwarf Korean' lilac and 'Adelaide Hood-less' and 'Lambert Closse' roses, the remainder of the plants will be repetitions of those in other beds. Daylilies will spill over slightly onto the path at the entrance to this garden.

The end product is a well-defined cottage-style garden with a mixture of strong forms and traditional plants. This landscape is very much in keeping with the scale and style of the house and, most importantly, the owners' desires.

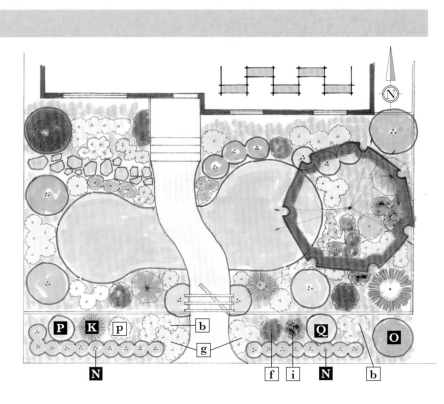

Shrubs

K Juniper 'Blue Arrow'
Juniperus scopulorum ....(1)

N Caragana 'Russian Globe'
Caragana frutex 'Globosa' ....(18)

O Lilac 'Dwarf Korean'
Syringa meyeri 'Palibin' ....(1)

P Rose 'Lambert Closse'
Rosa ....(1)

Q Rose 'Adelaide Hoodless'
Rosa ....(1)

Perennials

b Obedient Plant
Physostegia virginiana.............(6)

f Peony *Paeonia*............................(1)

g Daylily *Hemerocallis*.................(6)

i Blue Sage 'May Night'
Salvia x *sylvestris*.....................(1)

p False Sunflower 'Summer Sun'
Heliopsis helianthoides
var. *scabra*.................................(1)

A Modern Garden

Flat-roofed house, too much lawn, northern exposure

Wish List: bold lines, modern design and less lawn.

This home was built in the 1970s and stands out from the traditional-looking houses on the block. It was designed to maximize passive solar heating, so nearly all of its windows are on the south side of the house and face the backyard. Because the lone window at the front of the house didn't afford much of a view, the original owners kept the front landscaping to a minimum—a few shrubs and some lawn. The yard is well designed in that it has a walkway that allows for direct access to the front door, and a raised planter was cleverly positioned to visually break the expanse of concrete between the walkway and the driveway. The current owner enjoys gardening and wants a design that will complement the spare lines of the house. He also wants to eliminate much of the lawn.

Stage Two elevation

The Plan

Assessing the Design Options

The unique design of the home calls for a unique plan for the garden. The notion of minimalism brings to mind lots of hardscaping and a minimum number of plants. However, because the yard already has a mass of concrete and bare-bones plantings, putting in only a few plants would over-emphasize the austerity of the home. Therefore, to soften the yard's hard lines, while keeping with a minimalist approach, I recommended using lots of plants but limiting the number of varieties. Mimicking the straight lines of the house, the majority of the plants will also be planted in straight lines or at angles to each other. The homeowner will landscape in manageable stages so that he can prepare the planting beds properly.

Landscape Tip

Don't plant too close to your house. Far too many beautiful cedars have been either cruelly topped or completely removed because they have grown into the eaves. I've even seen a large spruce cover all the windows on an entire side of a house. Sure, the tree may keep the house cool and offer privacy, but how do the owners get in there to wash the windows or to paint? Cleaning the gutters of needles must be an annual chore. Besides being annoying, these situations can also create problems with house foundations.

A Modern Garden—Stage One

With the hardscaping elements already in place and good soil added to the beds, the eager owner can begin to plant. Starting in the foundation bed next to the front door, a 'Hicks' yew hedge will be planted—perfect for tolerating the bed's shady conditions. The hedge can be tip-pruned annually to keep it below the small front window. In front of the hedge, a block of 'Flaming Mound' spireas with red-tipped gold foliage in spring and bright fall colour will contrast with the dark green of the yews. The bluish flowers of 'Johnsons's Blue' cranesbill will look nice against the green-yellow summer colour of the spireas. Where this bed wraps around the house along the path to the back garden, I've selected 'Frances Williams' hostas. Their variegated leaves will glow in this dark, narrow spot. I have suggested that simple stepping stones be laid to lead to the faucet located behind the yews.

A line of 'Karl Foerster' feather reed grass planted in the bed along the driveway will define the edge of the property. Its strong architectural form will lend the garden the contemporary look the owner likes. In the rest of the driveway bed, 'Ruby Carousel' barberries will contrast well against the backdrop of the grasses. The barberries will also balance the spring and fall colour of the foundation bed spireas. One final addition, an upright, dense 'Moonglow' juniper, will partially hide the empty strip along the west wall of the garage.

Since the raised planter located between the driveway and the walkway won't provide plants with the winter protection they need, I've chosen to fill the space with annual fountain grass. It will look stunning in the summer and fall and will thrive in this location.

At the completion of this stage, the design of the yard is still stark, but mulch placed around the plants will add texture, and in a season or two, the plants will grow and fill the space.

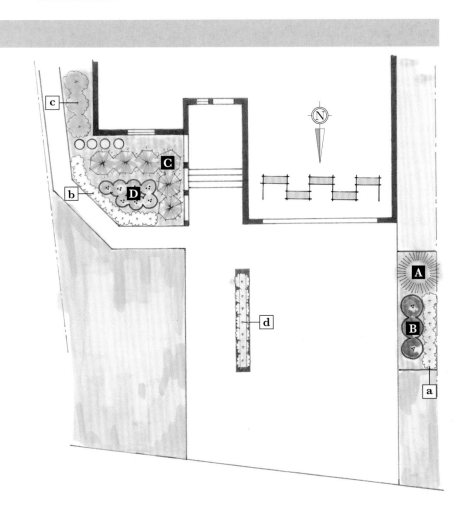

Trees

A Juniper 'Moonglow'
Juniperus scopulorum ....(1)

Shrubs

B Barberry 'Ruby Carousel'
Berberis thunbergii var.
atropurpurea 'Bailone' ....(3)

C Yew 'Hicks'
Taxus x *media* 'Hicksii'.............(6)

D Spirea 'Flaming Mound'
Spiraea japonica......................(7)

Perennials & Annuals

a Feather Reed Grass 'Karl Foerster'
Calamagrostis x *acutiflora*.......(6)

b Cranesbill 'Johnson's Blue'
Geranium...................................(9)

c Hosta 'Frances Williams'
Hosta...(3)

d Purple Fountain Grass (annual)
Pennisetum rubrum..................(7)

A Modern Garden—Stage Two

This stage of the design focuses on removing the tired lawn to create a large dramatic planting that extends toward the street.

A 'True North' linden, the most important vertical element in the design, has an upright habit that will keep it well within the bounds of the property. Lindens are attractive trees year round, and their sweetly scented flowers are loved by bees. To pull both sides of the yard together, I've chosen to repeat plantings. A second Moonglow juniper will be planted opposite the foundation bed to match the one along the driveway and will become the feature plant along the path to the back garden. Feather reed grass and barberries will grow along the property's eastern edge, mirroring the same combination along the opposite side of the property. A single 'Miss Kim' lilac in front of the linden will scent the garden in the spring and will even provide some fall colour. 'Icee Blue' junipers will repeat the Moonglow junipers' colour at the front of the yard. The 'Gold Star' junipers I've selected to grow near the linden will contrast with the blue junipers and reinforce, once more, the colour of the Flaming Mound spireas. Finally, the pink flowers of 'Brandon Pink' coralbells will add more colour to the bed edge nearest the public sidewalk.

With this last stage complete, the home's strong but simple architecture can be appreciated and it will look grounded within a simple, yet fully planted, garden.

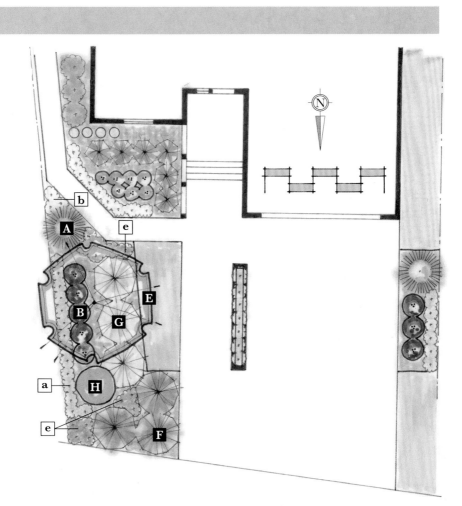

Trees

A Juniper 'Moonglow'
 Juniperus scopulorum ....(1)

E Linden 'True North'
 Tilia americana 'Duros' ....(1)

Shrubs

B Barberry 'Ruby Carousel'
 Berberis thunbergii var. *atropurpurea*
 'Bailone'....................................(5)

F Juniper 'Icee Blue' *Juniperus horizontalis*
 'Monber'....................................(3)

G Juniper 'Goldstar' *Juniperus chinensis*
 'Bakaurea'.................................(3)

H Lilac 'Miss Kim'
 Syringa patula ....(1)

Perennials

a Feather Reed Grass 'Karl Foerster'
 Calamagrostis x *acutiflora*......(14)

b Cranesbill 'Johnson's Blue'
 Geranium...................................(3)

e Coralbells 'Brandon Pink'
 Heuchera sanguinea ....(13)

A Native Garden

Overgrown and unnaturally
pruned shrubs, narrow front path,
Alberta location, western exposure

Wish List: butterflies and birds, easy maintenance
and a wider front path.

*The trees and shrubs on this 40-year-old property are over-
grown or pruned into unnatural-looking forms. Although the
deciduous plants could be rejuvenated in about three years,
the spruces are beyond reclamation. Rather than trying to
work around the existing plants, the homeowners, who are
drawn to natural-looking landscapes, have opted to start
fresh. They like the idea of having curved beds and are
interested in creating a space for butterflies and birds.
The sidewalk to their front door is straight and very narrow
(90cm wide), and there is a downspout that crosses the path
to the back garden. Budget considerations dictate that the
work will need to be completed in stages.*

Stage Three elevation

The Plan

Assessing the Design Options

Although this garden is designed with Alberta's native plants (and their relatives) in mind, the same design principles apply to all locations. To create a natural or native garden, topography must be considered. Raised areas, rock outcroppings and plants all play a part. The homeowners' desire for a bird-and-butterfly-friendly space will be reached with plants that provide shelter and food, and these plants, fortunately, have low water and fertilizer requirements, which will satisfy the "easy maintenance" request. Since going out to the bush to dig up plants is ill-advised and seed collection is often frowned upon, purchasing native species from a garden centre is the best plan of action.

A slightly curved, 1.4m wide path will be created to provide better access to the house. Rather than hauling away the soil removed to widen the path, it will be retained for use in the construction of a berm that will provide some topographical relief to the flat garden. I recommended adding large rocks within the berm to create the look of outcroppings, and using the downspout-hidden-by-an-arbour method to free up the path to the back garden.

Landscape Tip

Proper pruning involves two techniques: heading back (reducing the length of a branch by cutting it back to either an outward-facing bud or to a strong lateral branch) and thinning (removing an entire branch, either to a main branch or to the ground). A good rule is never to remove more than one third of the shrub per year. Shrubs that bloom on last year's wood should be pruned immediately after they flower. Shrubs that bloom on new wood should be pruned when they are dormant.

A Native Garden—Stage One

The first step is to install the walkway and create the berm area, which involves placing five boulders of varying size around the berm. Another boulder will be added on the other side of the yard, so the owners may want to purchase them all at once (see page 23 for tips on placing boulders in the garden). The homeowners can then begin to put a few plants in the foundation bed beside the front steps.

The first addition to this bed will be a row of 'Tor' spireas. Tor is a cultivated variety of a native birch-leaved spirea with white, flat-topped clusters of flowers in the summer and excellent foliage colour in the fall. The thin leaf sunflower 'Capenoch Star' planted by the steps will bloom from summer to fall with bright-yellow flowers—a butterfly draw. I've selected a bearded iris because the only iris native to Alberta is blue-eyed grass—a bit short for this space. Bearded iris is taller and just too tough and beautiful a plant to leave out. Native blue flax and the cultivated variety look virtually identical, but because native coral bells (*Heucheras*) are not particularly showy, I've substituted them with 'Brandon Pink' coralbells. The 'Blue Bird' clematis grown on the arbour over the side-walk at the side of the house, will look almost indistinguishable from its native counterpart. In front of this clematis, bog rosemary will flourish happily in the moist soil where the roof runoff exits the downspout.

With the completion of this stage, the landscape will have interesting topography, an attractive and safe pathway and a foundation bed filled with plants that will begin to attract wildlife and add colour.

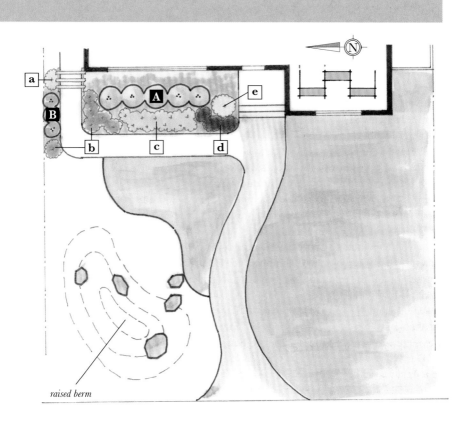

raised berm

Shrubs

A Spirea 'Tor'
   Spiraea betulifolia .... (5)

B Bog Rosemary 'Blue Ice'
   Andromeda polifolia .... (3)

Perennials

a Big Petal Clematis 'Blue Bird'
   Clematis macropetala .... (1)

b Coralbells 'Brandon Pink'
   Heuchera sanguinea .... (5) + (1)

c Perennial Blue Flax
   Linum perenne .... (9)

d Bearded Iris
   Iris germanica .... (3)

e Thin Leaf Sunflower
   'Capenoch Star' *Helianthus* .... (1)

A Native Garden—Stage Two

This stage of the design focuses on integrating the berm within a large planting bed on the property's north side. This bed widens toward the street.

For the top of the berm, I've selected a 'Midnight Schubert' chokecherry—a cultivated variety that's not supposed to sucker. Its dark-purple leaves will stand out well against the light-coloured house, and the clusters of fruit it produces is enjoyed by birds. A 'Wentworth' cranberry and a 'Wichita Blue' juniper will provide some height toward the back of the bed and will produce more berries and shelter for birds. Instead of planting native snowberries, which are not terribly ornamental, the very attractive 'Marleen' snowberry will be used at the berm's edge closest to the neighbours. Next to the snowberries, 'Dart's Red' spirea will be a showy substitute for native *Spiraea densiflora*, and plantings of 'Blueberry Delight' and 'Blue Prince' junipers will cover the curving middle area where the bed meets the lawn and sidewalks. Long-blooming 'Goldfinger' potentillas, planted next to the public sidewalk, will highlight the yellow siding of the house. The remaining perennials chosen for this bed will attract hummingbirds and butterflies.

With this side of the garden completed, the yard will look nice from inside the house but lopsided from the street. However, the results should provide plenty of motivation to proceed to the next step.

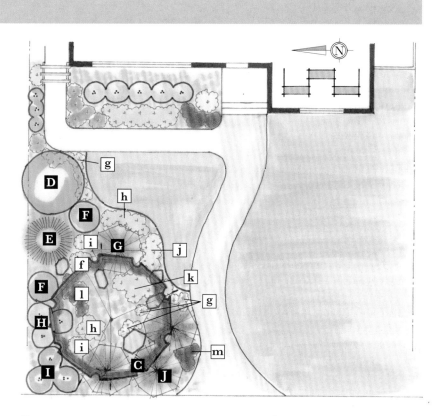

Trees

C Chokecherry 'Midnight Schubert'
   Prunus virginiana........................(1)

D Cranberry 'Wentworth'
   Viburnum trilobum......................(1)

E Juniper 'Wichita Blue'
   Juniperus scopulorum.................(1)

F Spirea 'Dart's Red'
   Spiraea japonica........................(2)

G Juniper 'Blueberry Delight'
   *Juniperus communis
   depressa 'Amidak'*.....................(1)

H Snowberry 'Marleen'
   *Symphoricarpos x
   doorenbosii*...............................(3)

I Potentilla 'Goldfinger'
   Potentilla fruticosa..................(3)

J 'Blue Prince' Juniper
   Juniperus horizontalis...............(3)

Perennials

f Beebalm 'Marshall's Delight'
   Monarda....................................(1)

g Greyleaf Cranesbill 'Ballerina'
   Geranium cinereum........(10) + (7)

h Creeping Speedwell 'Waterperry Blue'
   Veronica..........................(5) + (5)

i Liatris *Liatris spicata*...............(2)

j Blanket Flower 'Baby Cole'
   Gaillardia.................................(5)

k Cranesbill 'Johnson's Blue'
   Geranium...................................(5)

l Himalayan Fleece Flower
   'Darjeeling Red'
   Persicaria affinis......................(5)

m Prairie Crocus
   Pulsatilla patens.......................(3)

A Native Garden—Stage Three

This last stage of the design turns its attention to creating balance by installing a large planting bed on the opposite side of this front yard.

Including a large boulder to balance those in the berm opposite and repeating many of the plants from Stage Two will create unity in the garden. In the centre of this bed, a 'Black Hills' spruce—a slower growing variety of white spruce—will be an attractive specimen. It will be planted well away from the house to allow it to attain an even form and to prevent it from blocking the home's windows. A light-coloured 'Silver & Gold' dogwood, planted past the corner of the house, will extend the house colour into the planting bed. Directing the roof runoff towards the dogwood and beyond to the 'Dwarf Arctic' birches will provide the shrubs with additional water. An informal hedge of potentilla provides a background for this bed and defines the properties southernmost edge.

I selected a 'Blue Nest' spruce, which is a dwarf form of the native black spruce, to add an attractive blue-grey colour to the garden and to create a background for the boulder. In front of the boulder, blue-eyed grass will be planted, and because it self-sows readily, only one or two will need to be purchased.

Now the garden has a beautiful natural look, tamed to be low maintenance and to complement the home. With all of the stages complete, this front garden will welcome friends and fauna alike.

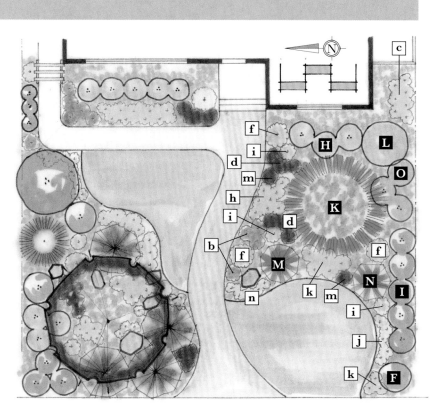

Trees

K Spruce 'Black Hills'
Picea glauca var. *densata* ....(1)

Shrubs

F Spirea 'Dart's Red'
Spiraea japonica ....(1)

H Snowberry 'Marleen' *Symphoricarpos*
x *doorenbosii* ....(3)

I Potentilla 'Goldfinger'
Potentilla fruticosa ....(5)

L Dogwood 'Silver & Gold'
Cornus sericea ....(1)

M Spruce 'Blue Nest'
Picea mariana 'Ericoides' ....(1)

N Juniper 'Green Carpet'
Juniperus communis ....(1)

O Birch 'Dwarf Arctic'
Betula nana ....(3)

Perennials

b Coralbells 'Brandon Pink'
Heuchera sanguinea ....(3) + (1)

c Perennial Blue Flax
Linum perenne ....(7)

d Bearded Iris
Iris germanica ....(3) + (3)

f Beebalm 'Marshall's Delight'
Monarda ....(1) + (1)

h Creeping Speedwell 'Waterperry Blue'
Veronica ....(8)

i Liatris
Liatris spicata ....(1) + (1)

k Cranesbill 'Johnson's Blue'
Geranium................................(5)

m Prairie Crocus
Pulsatilla patens ....(1) + (1)

n Blue-Eyed Grass
Sisyrinchium idahoense ....(1 or 2)

A Japanese Garden

Overgrown and dying trees,
hidden front door, 35-year-old bungalow,
northern exposure

Wish List: a Japanese-style garden, a seating area
and interesting features.

The homeowners purchased their 70s bungalow as a fixer-upper. Having finished the interior, they are now ready to get to work landscaping the front yard. Since their renovations reflect a clean-lined mission style, they are interested in creating a garden with a complementary Japanese theme. Luckily, the vertical wood cladding on the house is in keeping with a Japanese style. The homeowners want to do most of the work themselves, which means spreading it over two or three years, but will need to hire a tree removal service to create a blank slate and hire an electrician to run power to the water basin and lantern features.

Stage Three elevation

The Plan

Assessing the Design Options

An authentic Japanese garden has a set of rules that are quite rigid, but that doesn't mean the owners can't create a slightly more flexible version that is still inspired by this style. The L-shape of the house lends itself to the creation of a courtyard, a key element in a Japanese garden. Because the house faces north, most of the plantings will benefit from being distanced from the shade of the house. They will also provide a lovely background for the courtyard. The homeowners can put their skills to the test creating many of the hardscaping elements: a fence, a covered gate and a low deck. The boulders, statuary pieces and stepping stones can be purchased.

Landscape Tip

Having a water feature in your garden is a plus but may be problematic in a front yard. For safety reasons, it's best to install a pebble pool—one with a reservoir that is below ground level and that is covered by a layer of pebbles. In-ground pond kits can be purchased, or you can make your own using a sturdy plastic pail as the reservoir and some heavy wire mesh to support the pebbles.

A Japanese Garden—Stage One

Starting with the hardscape elements, the first order of business is to replace the tiny landing at the front door with a deck along the recessed face of the house, a version of *engawa*, which is part of a traditional Japanese home. The deck will be less than 60cm from the ground, so no railing is required according to my local building code, which means the view from the house won't be obscured. A 1.5m concrete path will lead the way to the front door, and within the courtyard, a path of flat stepping stones will be laid. I've designed the concrete path with a slight jog to create a little more interest. An open-work fence *(Yotsume-gaki)* will define the courtyard space, and a covered gate *(Niwa-mon)* will separate the public space from the private area.

Yukimi-gata

Japanese gardens usually aren't flat, so I suggest creating a bermed area, complete with boulders within the courtyard, backed by horizontal landscape ties and edged with short lengths of vertical ties (referred to as post edging). The soil from the excavation of the pathway will be used to create the berm. Finally, traditional Japanese elements, such as a snow-viewing lantern *(Yukimi-gata)* and a water basin *(Tsukubai)* can be placed to complete the courtyard.

Tsukubai

On the public side of the fence, a large bed gently undulates across the property. Two feature trees, a lodgepole pine and a 'Sensation' maple can be planted at this time since they will be well out of the way of construction. Square concrete pavers will be used to link the front path to the driveway. Lastly, a strip of lawn will frame the bed and bridge the space between the public sidewalk and the plantings to come.

Simple lantern in shoji style

At the end of this stage, the garden will look a bit bare of plants, but the deck, fence, gate and path will give balance to the yard.

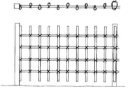

Yotsume-gaki

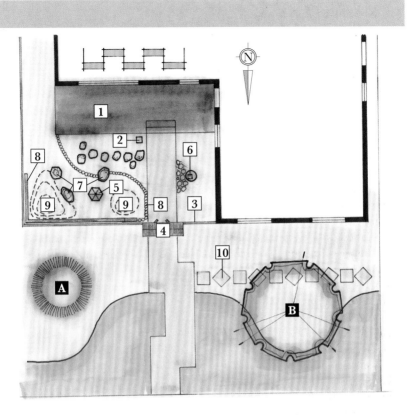

Trees

A Lodgepole Pine
  Pinus contorta var. *latifolia*......(1)

B Maple 'Sensation'
  Acer negundo..............................(1)

Hardscape Elements

1. *Engawa* or Japanese veranda. To be kept clear of potted plants, generally only chairs are on an *engawa*.

2. Simple lantern in *shoji* style.

3. *Yotsume-gaki*-style fence—traditionally made of bamboo. In our climate cedar, spruce or pine 1 x 1s are more durable.

4. Covered gate *(Niwa-mon)*.

5. Snow lantern *(Yukimi-gata)*.

6. *Tsukubai*—stone basin set within base of stones (60cm tall or less). A tea house entrance element.

7. Boulders and stepping stones—stepping stones will need to be set high to float above the "sea" of thyme to be planted in Stage Two.

8. Post edging and landscape ties around berm (10cm increase in grade).

9. Bermed area. Each broken line indicates 5cm increase in elevation.

10. 60cm x 60cm concrete pavers.

A Japanese Garden—Stage Two

With a wonderful Japanese garden-inspired foundation in place, serious planting can begin, starting with a 'Dwarf Korean' tree-form lilac and a 'Tannenbaum' pine, which are small enough for the confines of the courtyard. Although the other plantings I've selected for this space are not traditional, they will create a restful combination of colours and textures. To keep the stepping stones visible, the wooly thyme will have to be manicured occasionally.

I've selected the area outside of the courtyard, behind the maple, as the next spot to receive the owners' attention. A chokeberry hedge and a wayfaring tree will begin to add balance to that side of the house. 'Autumn Magic' chokeberries are not only attractive year-round but also more open-looking than other types of hedges. The hedge will be planted a good distance from the house. This is to prevent the chokeberries from receiving too much shade from the overhang of the roof. The wayfaring tree has a lovely form and multiple seasons of interest.

At this stage of completion, the garden takes on an almost modern Asian feel.

Trees

C Lilac 'Dwarf Korean'
   Syringa meyeri
   'Palibin' (tree form) ....(1)

D Pine 'Tannenbaum'
   Pinus mugo ....(1)

Shrubs

E Barberry 'Concorde'
   Berberis thunbergii
   var. atropurpurea ....(1)

F Dogwood 'Kesselring'
   Cornus alba 'Kesselringii' ....(1)

G Cedar 'Holmstrup'
   Thuja occidentalis ....(3)

H Potentilla 'Nuuk'
   Potentilla tridentata ....(5)

I Cranberry 'Bailey Compact'
   Viburnum trilobum ....(1)

J Maple 'Emerald Elf'
   Acer tataricum ssp. ginnala ....(1)

K Wayfaring Tree 'Mohican'
   Viburnum lantana ....(1)

L Chokeberry 'Autumn Magic' ....
   Aronia melanocarpa ....(10)

M Dwarf Balsam Fir
   Abies balsamea 'Nana' ....(1)

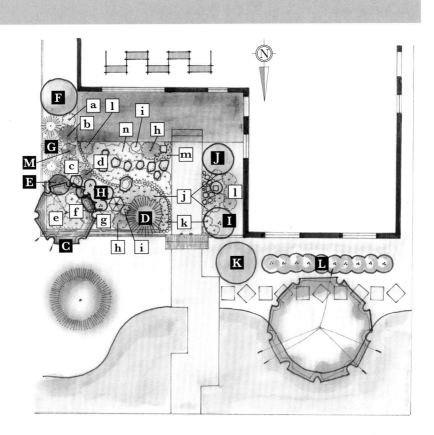

Perennials

a Feather Reed Grass 'Overdam'
  Calamagrostis x *acutiflora*........(1)

b Purple Bugbane
  Actaea simplex ....(1)

c Coralbells 'Strawberry Candy'
  Heuchera ....(5)

d Dwarf Bearded Iris 'Boo'
  Iris..(1)

e Daylily 'Hyperion'
  Hemerocallis.............................(5)

f Lamb's Ear
  Stachys byzantina.....................(3)

g Feather Reed Grass 'Karl Foerster'
  Calamagrostis x *acutiflora*.......(3)

h Peony 'Coral Charm'
  Paeonia ....(1) + (1)

i Liatris 'Kobold'
  Liatris spicata ....(1) + (1)

j Heartleaf Bergenia
  Bergenia cordifolia (5) + (3) + (1)

k Cranesbill 'New Dimension'
  Geranium........................(4) + (3)

l Solomon's Seal
  Polygonatum...................(3) + (1)

m Blue Fescue 'Elijah Blue'
  Festuca glauca ....(5)

n Wooly Thyme
  Thymus pseudolanuginosus.....(13)

A Japanese Garden—Stage Three

The final stage of this design is devoted to finishing off the area outside the courtyard fence.

Another hedge of chokeberries will be located just outside the fence to mirror the one on the opposite side of the yard. It will increase the sense of enclosure and create continuity in the garden. This shrub also offers intense fall colour. Nestled beneath and around the lodgepole pine planted in Stage One are 'Mops' pine, 'Magic Carpet' spirea, 'New Dimension' cranesbill, daylilies and 'Miss Kim' lilac.

Across the yard, under and around Stage One's Sensation maple, grasses are added among the spirea, cranesbill and daylilies to create movement. A groundcover of heartleaf bergenia and a 'Pumila' spruce will also be added and will look good all year. The additional plantings of the shrubs and perennials I've chosen will provide a variety of colour and texture.

The completed design is a modern, colourful version of a Japanese-style garden that is fairly easy to maintain.

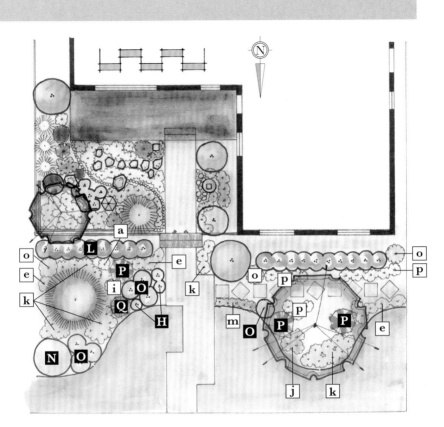

Shrubs

H Potentilla 'Nuuk'
Potentilla tridentata................ (3)

L Chokeberry 'Autumn Magic'
Aronia melanocarpa.................. (9)

N Lilac 'Miss Kim'
Syringa patula .... (1)

O Spirea 'Magic Carpet'
Spiraea japonica.... (3) + (3) + (1)

P Spruce 'Pumila'
Picea abies...............(1) + (1) + (1)

Q Pine 'Mops'
Pinus mugo................................. (1)

Perennials

a Feather Reed Grass 'Overdam'
Calamagrostis x acutiflora ......(1)

e Daylily 'Hyperion'
Hemerocallis.......... (3) + (5) + (1)

i Liatris 'Kobold'
Liatris spicata .... (1)

j Heartleaf Bergenia
Bergenia cordifolia................... (3)

k Cranesbill 'New Dimension'
Geranium..... (5) + (3) + (5) + (8)

m Blue Fescue 'Elijah Blue'
Festuca glauca .... (5)

o Goat's Beard *Aruncus
dioicus* 'Kneiffii' .....(1) + (1) + (1)

p Bishop's Hat *Epimedium
x rubrum*................ (3) + (5) + (3)

Xeriscape

Small front yard, worn out lawn, eastern exposure

Wish List: no lawn and a
low-maintenance but attractive yard.

*While the owners of this home were driving around looking
for a new house prior to buying this one, they saw a few front
gardens that had shrubs and perennials instead of lawn. They
liked this style a lot, so when they purchased their home,
they decided to replace the tired worn out lawn with plants.
Since more than half the yard is taken up by the paved drive,
they hoped it wouldn't take too much effort to landscape the
remaining space. Although they were both quite enthusiastic
about the idea of creating a xeriscaped front garden, the pros-
pect of not having a lawn to mow was especially appealing to
the husband.*

Landscape Tip

Roots will grow only where
there is water, so a deep
watering is more beneficial
for your plants than is a
frequent shallow watering.
The rule of thumb is that
you will need **at least** 5L
of water for every 30cm
of height or spread of the
plant. This will ensure that
the entire rootball, plus the
surrounding soil, will be wet.

The Plan

Assessing the Design Options

What is a xeriscape? One thing it isn't is a zero-scape with nothing but rocks and a few shrubs. Xeriscaping is a creative landscaping approach to water conservation and involves minimizing the use of tap water by decreasing turf. Soil improvement and appropriate plant selection are also important principles associated with xeriscaping.

Because the homeowners are not enamored with the idea of having a front lawn, the concept of xeriscaping works well for them. One of our prime considerations is to ensure that the soil in the front yard can support the growth of the required plant material. This will mean the removal of a portion of the clay subsoil to allow for a minimum of 30cm of quality topsoil to be spread over the entire side of the yard where planting will take place. The utilities must be located prior to excavation. To minimize runoff, the ideal depth of the excavation is one that, after the topsoil is brought in, allows for a finished grade just below the edges of the driveway and sidewalk.

Once the excavation is completed, the problem of the compacted clay subsoil must be addressed. The homeowners will need to spread a 5 to 7.5cm-deep layer of compost over the area and till it thoroughly into the clay. This will allow for better drainage and root penetration. Once done, the topsoil can be brought in and spread by hand, so as not to undo the previous work.

Completed elevation

Xeriscape

Although I've created a landscape plan that can be completed in one year, the homeowners can work in stages by planting the tree and the shrubs the first year and the perennials the following year. The path of stepping stones to the storage area along the side of the house can be placed before the plants go into the garden.

The silvery foliage of the Russian olive I've selected will stand out well against the dark siding. When viewed from the house, the green of the 'Idyllwild' juniper will contrast well against the silver of the Russian olive. 'Wilton's Blue Rug' junipers will serve as ground cover, growing low and spreading relatively quickly. They will also colour a purplish tinge in the fall. At the front corner of the lot, a 'Coppertina' ninebark will add strong colour to the garden and balance out the strong colour of the house. The ground-covering perennials in the plan will all flower at different times over the growing season and create a variety of textures and colours. 'Pygmy' caraganas are tough plants that will line the driveway and keep people from cutting across the property.

This design, once the plants have established, will mimic those the owner's have admired.

Trees

A Russian Olive
Elaegnus angustifolia ....(1)

Shrubs

B Juniper 'Idyllwild'
Juniperus virginiana ....(1)

C Spirea 'Fairy Queen'
Spiraea trilobata ....(1)

D Potentilla 'Pink Beauty'
Potentilla fruticosa ....(3)

E Lilac 'Miss Kim'
Syringa patula ....(1)

F Pine 'Slowmound'
Pinus mugo ....(1)

G Juniper 'Wilton's Blue Rug'
Juniperus horizantalis
'Wiltonii' ....(5)

H Pine 'White Bud'
Pinus mugo ....(1)

I Honeysuckle 'Emerald Mound'
Lonicera xylosteum ....(1)

J Ninebark 'Coppertina'
Physocarpus opulifolius
'Mindia' ....(1)

K Caragana 'Pygmy'
Caragana pygmaea ....(9)

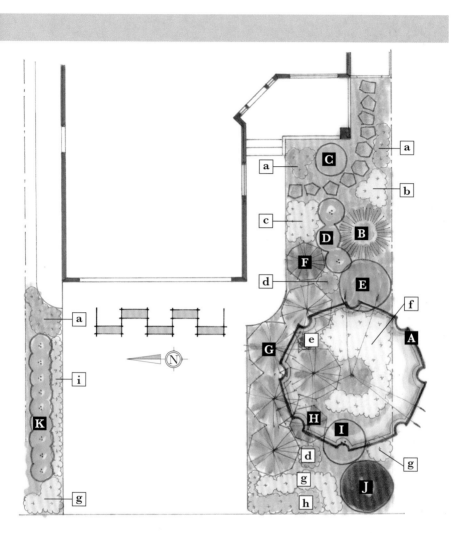

Perennials

a Heartleaf Bergenia *Bergenia cordifolia* .... (5) + (3) + (3)

b Feather Reed Grass 'Overdam' *Calamagrostis x acutiflora*....... (3)

c Mother of Thyme *Thymus serpyllum*..................... (8)

d Peony *Paeonia* ....(1) + (1)

e Stonecrop 'Matrona' *Sedum telephium*...................... (1)

f Bigroot Cranesbill *Geranium macrorrhorizum* ....(14)

g Daylily *Hemerocallis*.......... (3) + (5) + (1)

h Stonecrop *Sedum* .... (9)

i Creeping Speedwell *Veronica oltensis*...................... (9)

Spicing It Up

Existing plants, indirect access
to front door, western exposure

Wish List: interesting plantings, a second pathway
and a softened deck edge.

The homeowners have already done a fair bit of work to this
front yard, including installing a new path from the house
to the driveway and building a front deck on which to enjoy
the afternoon sun. They are justifiably pleased with the work
they have done but feel they could go a bit further. They think
a second path is needed and would like to add some plantings
would create interest through the seasons and help the deck
to fit into the landscape. They would like to accomplish this
work in one stage.

Landscape Tip

Use a water-soluble fertilizer
once a month beginning when
the ground warms in the spring
and continue until the beginning
of August. After August 1, your
lawn, herbaceous perennials
and your trees and shrubs need
to slow down new growth in
order to harden off before
winter.

The Plan

Assessing the Design Options

The homeowners are on the way to a very nice landscape, but they made one serious error: limbing up the spruce in front of their house in hopes of growing a better lawn underneath it. Unfortunately, this really only creates an unsightly area where next to nothing will grow. Rather than battling the difficult growing conditions the spruce poses, it's better to just let a spruce's branches drape close to the ground, get rid of the lawn beneath and around it and then cover the soil with mulch.

The owners have good instincts. An extra pathway from the street to the front steps is definitely in order, and they have decided to do this before the beds are created. Having the path curve gently will complement the curve of the planting beds I propose. In particular, the addition of a bed on the spruce side of the walkway will create more interest on the side of the house that right now has little to draw the eye. But before the beds are created and the planting begins, a poorly placed cedar in front of a window will have to be removed. All of the plantings will build off the work that the homeowners have done.

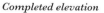

Completed elevation

Spicing It Up

Softening the low deck by surrounding it with plants is the first task to tackle. A 'Dart's Gold' ninebark, a 'Rock/Ground' cotoneaster and some daylilies planted around the base of the deck will enclose its edges nicely.

Next, the bed surrounding the limbed up spruce and extending all the way to the home's foundation should be created. A 'Snowball' viburnum and an 'Emerald Triumph' wayfaring tree I've selected for planting on either side of window have white blossoms in the spring. Planting them on either side of the window will shade the walls in the summer but allow sun through in the winter. Solomon's seal will perform well in the shade between the shrubs and gradually fill the space. The addition of spireas and a 'Calgary Carpet' juniper combined with daylilies and veronica will fill the extra planting space along the new path and provide texture and colour. Bigroot cranesbill is a vigorous groundcover that can be added beneath the spruce at this stage. In time, the cranesbill may self-sow closer to the trunk and fill the space.

The final bed to be installed in front of the driveway sidewalk will separate the deck from the street, making the homeowners feel a little less exposed. A 'Muckle' plum is a small tree that will provide an exceptional display of pink blossoms in the spring and lovely fall colour. The other reason I selected a Muckle plum for this spot is that the flowers are sterile, meaning it will not produce berries that drop on the walk or driveway. The spireas and the juniper in this bed will be quasi repetitions of the shrubs on the other side of the walk. The daylilies also repeat those at the base of the deck, visually linking both sides of the path.

It's really not that difficult to spice up a tired landscape and, should the owners develop a keen taste for more spice, they can easily expand the beds until only a little—or no—lawn remains.

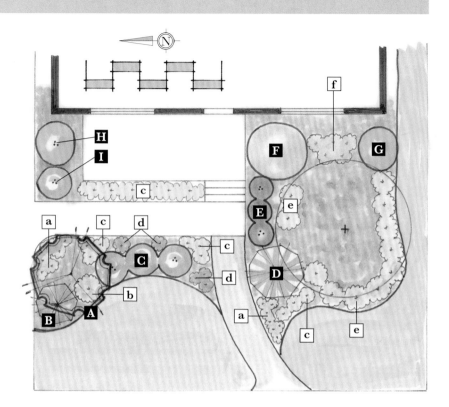

Trees

A Flowering Plum 'Muckle'
Prunus x *nigrella* ....(1)

Shrubs

B Juniper 'Blueberry Delight'
*Juniperus communis
depressa* 'Amidak' ....(1)

C Spirea 'Pink Parasols'
Spiraea fritschiana 'Wilma' .....(3)

D Juniper 'Calgary Carpet'
Juniperus sabina 'Monna' ....(1)

E Spirea 'Dart's Red'
Spiraea japonica ....(3)

F Viburnum 'Snowball'
Viburnum opulus 'Roseum' ....(1)

G Wayfaring Tree 'Emerald Triumph'
Viburnum lantana ....(1)

H Ninebark 'Dart's Gold'
Physocarpus opulifolius ....(1)

I Cotoneaster 'Rock/Ground'
Cotoneaster horizontalis var.
Perpusillus ....(1)

Perennials

a Creeping Speedwell
Veronica oltensis ....(7) + (7)

b Peony *Paeonia* ....(1)

c Daylily *Hemerocallis*
.....................(3) + (3) + (3) +(6)

d Coralbells
Heuchera ....(1) + (1) + (3)

e Bigroot Cranesbill
Geranium macrorrhizum .... (11)

f Solomon's Seal
Polygonatum............................. (5)

Tying It Together

Haphazard look, narrow path to house,
low-impact planting, eastern exposure

Wish List: wider path to house,
structured beds and a welcoming entrance.

*The homeowners have given landscaping their front garden a
noble effort—planting a number of trees and shrubs to relieve
the expanse of lawn—however, after assessing their work,
they feel that their front garden is missing something. The
good news is they have maintained grass-free areas around
the bases of the trees and shrubs, which has spared the plants
from lawnmower and weed-whacker damage.*

The Plan

Assessing the Design Options

The landscaping that the homeowners completed prior to this project can be
considered Stage One of this design. The Amur maples, 'Pyramidal' mountain
ash, pincherry and alpine currants they planted are suitable for a city lot and
are fairly well spaced. The plant material under the living room window (south
side of house) was also chosen well and, therefore, can remain. The perennials
on the opposite side were planted under the overhang of the roof and are suf-
fering from drought. They also developed a decided lean due to lack of light,
so removing them is the best option.

The first thing I recommended the owners do to make
the home's entrance more welcoming is widen the narrow,
concrete-slab path to the
front door to 1.4m and add a
small landing at the bottom
of the front steps. Adding
two large beds on either side
of the path will make the
existing plantings appear
more structured.

Completed elevation

Landscape Tip

The minimum width for a primary pathway is 1.4m. Anything less requires people to walk single file. A pathway with a bit of a lateral slope ensures that water drains to the sides, lessening icy conditions in winter. Unlike paths that me-ander through garden beds, paths to doors should be direct. There are lots of construction materials, but my preference is for paving stones. In my part of the country, concrete paths crack no matter how well they are prepared and poured. If problems occur with a paving stone path, only the part that needs fixing needs to be removed.

Tying It Together

Once the new path is completed, the home-owners can begin to mark out large, well-defined beds around the existing trees and shrubs. These beds will visually connect those plants and provide a place to grow more shrubs and perennials.

In the north bed, 'Fairy Queen' spireas will replace the perennials. Planted at a proper distance from the roof's overhang, the spireas won't have to reach for sunlight and, therefore, will maintain their natural form. A nest spruce and a selection of perennials will fill the space closest to the steps with interesting textures and colours. A little farther from the house, a 'Cream Cracker' dogwood will pop with colour against the dark green of the alpine currants. A 'Slowmound' mugo pine backed with a stand of 'Overdam' feather reed grass and combined with 'Johnson's Blue' geraniums and a 'Brandon Pink' coralbell will create a vignette that can be enjoyed from the front steps.

On the south side of the pathway, a second, large island bed will be created to enclose the existing plant material and to house a few new shrubs and perennials. Repeating plantings of perennials that appear in the other bed will visually link the beds on each side of the walkway. The addition of two 'Goldmound' spireas and some 'Blueberry Delight' junipers will give this bed an extra shot of colour.

With the design complete, the new, large, well-defined beds that incorporate the original planting beds will look lush, structured and welcoming. Without a bunch of tiny circles to mow around, the lawn will be easier to care for, too.

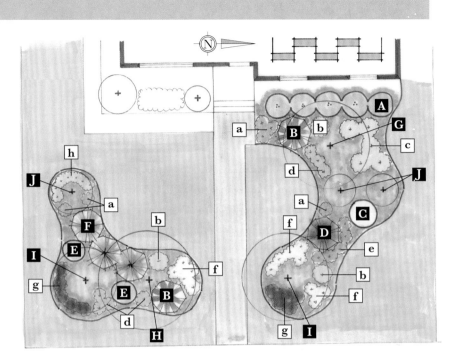

Existing Trees & Shrubs

G Pincherry
Prunus pensylvanica ....(1)

H Mountain Ash 'Pyramidal'
Sorbus ....(1)

I Amur Maple
Acer tataricum ssp. *ginnala* .....(2)

J Alpine Currant
Ribes alpina ....(3)

Shrubs

A Spirea 'Fairy Queen'
Spiraea trilobata ....(5)

B Nest Spruce
Picea abies 'Nidiformis' ....(2)

C Dogwood 'Cream Cracker'
Cornus alba ....(1)

D Pine 'Slowmound'
Pinus mugo ....(1)

E Spirea 'Goldmound'
Spiraea japonica ....(2)

F Juniper 'Blueberry Delight'
*Juniperus communis
depressa* 'Amidak' ....(3)

Perennials

a Coralbells 'Brandon Pink' *Heuchera
sanguinea* ....(3) + (1) + (1) + (1)

b Daylily
Hemerocallis ....(1) + (1) + (1)

c Hosta *Hosta* ....(5)

d Blue Oat Grass *Helictotrichon
sempervirens* ....(3) + (3) + (1)

e Feather Reed Grass 'Overdam'
Calamagrostis x acutiflora ....(5)

f Cranesbill 'Johnson's Blue'
Geranium ....(5) + (5) + (3)

g Heartleaf Bergenia
Bergenia cordifolia ....(5) + (5)

h Thyme *Thymus* ....(7)

Protecting Trees

Difficult to maintain lawn around
base of trees, northern exposure

Wish List: easy-to-mow lawn
and healthy trees.

*I happened by this arrangement of 'Swedish Columnar'
aspens one day and took a picture so that I could illustrate
a common problem people deal with in their yards: nicely
placed and spaced rows of trees that are hard to mow
around. Not only does mowing become a nuisance in this
situation, it also becomes dangerous to the health of the trees
if they are continually damaged by bumps or lacerations.
I also feel that the trees aren't shown to their best advantage
when not given a proper bed to anchor them.*

Landscape Tip

Almost every gardener makes
the mistake of choosing plants
with the wrong light requirements.
Before I knew better, I planted a
'Cuthbert Grant' rose in front of
my house. At face value, there is
nothing wrong with that, but our
house faces east and, at the time,
we had a stand of native poplars
shading the front yard. The rose
struggled in the poor light conditions for a couple of years before
I accidentally killed the poor
thing when trying to rid it of aphids—a case of second-degree herbicide. Had
I planted it in the backyard, where it would have received enough sun, there
would have been a happier ending.

The Plan

Assessing the Design Options

A simple solution for these homeowners is to use glyphosate to kill the lawn and perennial weeds around the trees (while, of course, protecting the trees from overspray) and to cover the dead grass with shredded bark or wood chips. This would create a clean, finished look, but wouldn't make much of an impression. A second option is to kill the lawn and perennial weeds around the trees using the same method and to then fill the space with plantings and mulch. I like the second option best because it would add a visual punch and would hide the unused space at the side of the house.

Completed elevation

Protecting Trees

Once the lawn is removed (see page 180 for a thorough explanation of the method), a bed surrounding the trees can be created. When it comes to planting around rows of trees, it's best to buy shrubs and perennials that come in small pots. A small rootball means a small planting hole, and a small hole means less disturbance to the roots of the aspens.

A 'Siberian' dogwood with solid deep-green foliage will look nice at the corner of the house and will utilize the runoff from the roof. Because the corner is shaded by the house and the aspens, choosing a variegated dogwood wouldn't have been a good idea. Only a portion of a variegated leaf contains chlorophyll, so the limited energy from the sun would cause the shrub to struggle. As understorey shrubs, snowberries are well adapted to lower light levels, and a nest spruce should perform well next to the aspens in the dappled afternoon shade. The addition of shade-loving perennials will complete the look and create some textural appeal. I have selected Bethlehem sage, goat's beard and hostas.

Keeping an area around trees free of grass and topping the soil with shredded bark or wood chips is a simple way to protect trees from mower damage—but it's not very exciting looking.

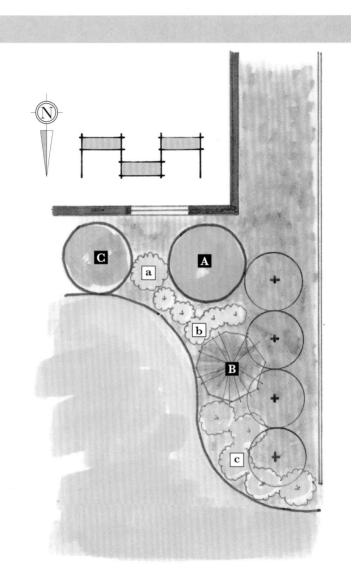

Shrubs

A Dogwood 'Siberian'
   Cornus alba 'Sibirica' ....(1)

B Nest Spruce
   Picea abies 'Nidiformis' ....(1)

C Snowberry 'Marleen'
   Symphoricarpos x *doorenbosii* ..(1)

Perennials

a Goat's Beard 'Kneiffii'
   Aruncus dioicus ....(1)

b Bethlehem Sage 'Argentea'
   Pulmonaria saccharata ....(5)

c Hosta *Hosta* ....(5)

Minimizing Utilities

Utility box on property, boring landscape,
no direct access to front door, western exposure

Wish List: disguise the utility box,
increase the resale value of the home
and create a new path.

*The homeowners have lived in their house for a number of
years and, up until now, have had little interest in landscaping the front yard. The plantings they do have in front of the
living room window are simple and well maintained. The
homeowners plan on retiring in ten years, and selling their
home is part of their plan for the future. Knowing that a nice
landscape will increase the value of the property, they figure
they might as well make the improvements now so they can
enjoy them for a while. Disguising the unattractive utility box
at the front of the lot is part of the plan. They are prepared to
do the work in one season.*

Landscape Tip

Planting too close to a fence or
property line can be problematic.
You may love the fruit from your
apple tree, but that doesn't mean
your neighbours will love picking
it up before they mow their lawn.
Canopies expand in width with
age, so planting a large tree
within 60 or 90cm of a fence is
not always neighbourly. Besides,
your neighbours have the right to
remove branches that grow over
to their property, which could
have ugly results in more ways
than one.

The Plan

Assessing the Design Options

A new path to the front door from the street will help visitors navigate their way to the house. The original path that went along the driveway can then become a secondary path. Modifying it with a flare at the driveway end will enlarge the area, making it easier to pass a vehicle without brushing up against it. A generous U-shaped planting bed will run along the gable end of the house, down the property line toward the street and along the public sidewalk. This bed will give some needed weight to the north side of the property and incorporate the existing elm. An existing foundation bed between the steps and the driveway can remain. Finally, a small bed will be created in front of the modified path to the driveway. The plantings in this bed will give the living room a bit of privacy from the street and the homeowners a pleasant view from the house.

Completed elevation

Minimizing Utilities

The first step in this stage is to have the pathways installed and the beds created. The contractor will save the excavated topsoil to supplement the soil in the new beds.

A cotoneaster hedge will be planted around the utility box to improve the view from the house. However, before a shovel can be put into the ground, utility lines will have to be located and planting regulations will need to be checked. When planting around a utility box, it's important to keep the area easily accessible for servicing. Therefore, the hedge will be planted approximately 1m from the edge of the box. This will allow for a 90cm wide hedge with a 60cm clear space around the utility box. A block of 'Calgary Carpet' junipers will be situated to the south of the hedge, beneath the elm, and a block of weigelas will be planted on its east side. The hedge will offer the weigelas wind protection.

At the corner of this bed, where the hedge meets the property line, a 'Black Beauty' elder will be planted. A row of 'Pink Parasols' spireas along the property line will complement the blossoms on the elder and will provide a strong show of colour in the fall. Carpathian bellflowers will add a splash of brightness. In the corner of the bed nearest the house, I've planned a path of stepping stones to lead to a small storage area along the side of the house. 'Pumila' spruce and heartleaf bergenias will fill the space along the foundation, completing this bed.

The second, smaller bed can now be planted. A 'Tannenbaum' pine positioned in front of the living room window will become a focal point throughout the year (without blocking the window), and the rich-pink flowers of a 'Morden Centennial' rose will be a striking feature in the summer. Junipers and perennials will fill the rest of this bed.

Once completed, the design will have perked up the front of the house, concealed the drab utility box and separated the homeowners' lot from that of their neighbours— all while adding value to this home.

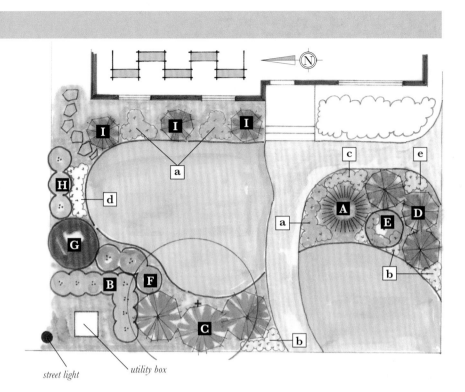

street light   utility box

Trees

A Pine 'Tannenbaum'
   Pinus mugo.................................(1)

Shrubs

B Cotoneaster 'Hedge/Peking'
   Cotoneaster acutifolius...........(8)

C Juniper 'Calgary Carpet'
   Juniperus sabina 'Monna'.........(3)

D Juniper 'Blueberry Delight'
   *Juniperus communis
   depressa 'Amidak'*..............(3)

E Rose 'Morden Centennial'
   Rosa..(1)

F Weigela 'Minuet'
   Weigela florida..........................(3)

G Elder 'Black Beauty'
   Sambucus nigra 'Gerda'.............(1)

H Spirea 'Pink Parasols'
   Spiraea fritschiana 'Wilma'.....(3)

I Spruce 'Pumila'
   Picea abies................................(3)

Perennials

a Heartleaf Bergenia *Bergenia
   cordifolia*..............(3) + (3) + (5)

b Mother of Thyme
   Thymus..................(5) + (7) + (3)

c Carpathian Bellflower 'Blue Clips'
   Campanula carpatica................(5)

d Carpathian Bellflower 'White Clips'
   Campanula carpatica f. alba.....(7)

e Russian Stonecrop
   Sedum kamtschaticum.............(3)

Failing Grades

Change in grade from front door to public sidewalk,
awkwardly spaced steps and path,
southern exposure
Wish List: address the grade, keep the large spruce
and have a low-maintenance yard.

The homeowners run a day home in their 40-year-old house
and need the front entrance to be child and parent friendly.
This means the front path must be able to accommodate
baby strollers as well as wheelchairs. The homeowners have
budgeted for a contractor to replace the sidewalk to the front
door and around to the back entrance. Because their money
is tied up in the sidewalk, they would like a plan that can be
completed in stages. They would also like to keep the large
spruce to save money—and because they love it.

Landscape Tip

It's hard to imagine that a skinny oak sapling in a #5 pot will grow into a 20m tall and 10m wide tree—but it will, so plan carefully. If you think you can keep a tree's size in check by topping it or hacking it back, you're mistaken: interfering with the tree's natural form will destroy its structural integrity and create an unnatural-looking, ugly and potentially dangerous tree.

Stage Two elevation

The Plan

Assessing the Design Options

I advised the owners that the pathway would need to have a strong, wide curve to provide the additional length needed to allow for a gradual slope. This gentle slope will eliminate the need for steps. Luckily for the homeowners, their large spruce was well placed and can be kept. However, because it is a bit ratty looking and has dead branches, it will need tidying up. In my plan, much of the lawn area beneath the spruce will be eliminated, and the remainder will be delineated by wide curves that will draw attention toward the front door. This will help create an easy to maintain yard with less lawn to fertilize, water and mow. A second, informal stepping stone path will also be added to create access to a gate leading to the back garden. I have broken the design into two stages but have pointed out natural places where they can be sub-divided, should the homeowners need to stretch out the stages.

Failing Grades—Stage One

Once the contractor completes the construction of the new main pathway, I suggest that the owners begin the landscaping by creating a new bed on the yard's west side, opposite the spruce. If they have to stop after this bed is completed, the yard will still appear balanced and colourful.

The east bed starts with the placement of two upright 'Montana Green' junipers on either side of the stepping stone path to the back garden. The junipers' presence will visually anchor the house to the surrounding landscape. The white flowers of the potentillas, which will be planted beneath the living room window, will stand out nicely against the brick finish of this side of the house. A 'Dwarf Korean' lilac planted beside one of the upright junipers will create nice contrast, and a pincherry tree will provide lovely four-season interest—clusters of white flowers in the spring, followed by red fruit, beautiful fall colour and striking, glossy bark in winter. A planting of blue flax beneath the tree will provide long-term interest through the summer. The flax self-sows freely, so a few plants can yield many more over time. A 'Pumila' spruce, 'Elijah Blue' fescue and a single peony round out the planting.

On the opposite side of the yard, a second bed will frame the spruce. Planting a 'Coppertina' ninebark and a 'Soongoricus' cotoneaster along the property line will screen the side-yard pathway, and 'Gold Lace' junipers will be nestled into the curve of the new path. A few daylilies and mass plantings of bigroot cranesbills will finish the bed and fill the area around the mature spruce. Both can be easily divided to create more plants.

The yard now meets all the requirements laid out by the homeowners. It is now accessible, welcoming and filled with unfussy plants. To take the design even further, they can pursue Stage Two as time and budget allow.

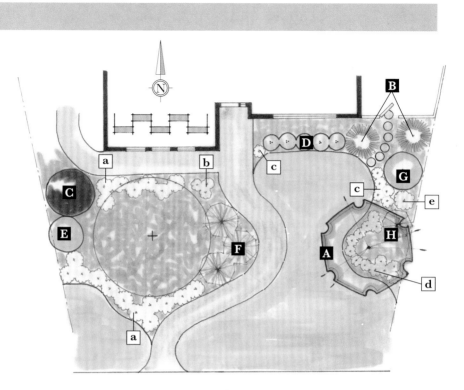

Trees

A Pincherry
   Prunus pensylvanica ....(1)

B Juniper 'Montana Green'
   Juniperus scopulorum ....(2)

Shrubs

C Ninebark 'Coppertina'
   Physocarpus opulifolius
   'Mindia'.......................................(1)

D Potentilla 'Abbotswood'
   Potentilla fruticosa..................(5)

E Cotoneaster 'Soongoricus'
   Cotoneaster racemiflorus
   var. soongoricus.........................(1)

F Juniper 'Gold Lace'
   Juniperus chinensis
   'Aurea' v Gold Lace ....(3)

G Lilac 'Dwarf Korean'
   Syringa meyeri 'Palibin'............(1)

H Spruce 'Pumila' *Picea abies* .....(1)

Perennials

a Bigroot Cranesbill
   Geranium macrorrhizum ....(19)

b Daylily 'Hyperion'
   Hemerocallis............................ (3)

c Fescue 'Elijah Blue'
   Festuca glauca .... (6)

d Perennial Blue Flax
   Linum perenne..........................(13)

e Peony *Paeonia*.............................(1)

Failing Grades—Stage Two

In this final stage, I propose the creation of a third planting area. Adding an island bed to the front of this yard, along the public pathway, will provide the homeowners with a pleasant view from their living room and eliminate more lawn. A strong focal point will be achieved with a 'Weeping' caragana, and richly coloured 'Ruby Carousel' barberries will be placed in an arc, mirroring the canopy of this dwarf tree. A single 'Abbotswood' potentilla and a 'Hyperion' daylily will visually connect the bed to the plantings near the house. A grouping of 'Blue Forest' junipers will add colour, and low-growing perennials will create an appealing carpet. Another path of stepping stones (preferably created using the same type of stepping stones as the path already in place) will provide a shortcut and the opportunity to stroll through the garden. All the plants in this bed are drought tolerant and will offer long-term, four-season interest.

This landscape will continue to be low-maintenance, especially if the owners follow my advice to mulch the beds and keep up on basic annual pruning tasks. It will also continue to be budget-friendly by using divisions of many of the perennials for the backyard.

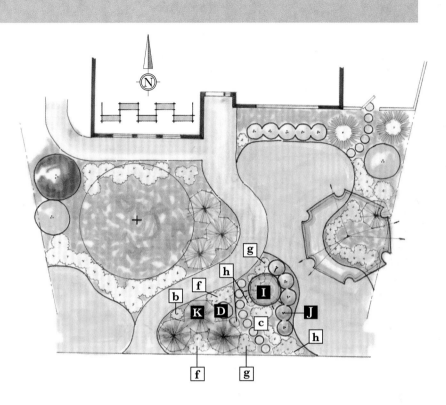

Trees

D Potentilla 'Abbotswood'
Potentilla fruticosa..................(1)

I Caragana 'Weeping'
Caragana arborescens
'Pendula' ....(1)

J Barberry 'Ruby Carousel'
Berberis thunbergii
var. *atropurpurea* 'Bailone' ......(5)

K Juniper 'Blue Forest'
Juniperus sabina.......................(3)

Perennials

b Daylily 'Hyperion '
Hemerocallis..............................(1)

c Fescue 'Elijah Blue'
Festuca glauca ....(5)

f Mother of Thyme
Thymus serpyllum.....................(3)

g Wooly Speedwell
Veronica armena ....(5)

h Hen and Chicks
Sempervivum.............................(5)

Postage Stamp Paradise

Tiny condominium lot, imposing fence,
northern exposure

Wish List: a patio and a low-maintenance garden.

*The homeowners are a young couple, and this property is
their starter home. The condo units have no back gardens so
the fronts are part of each owner's property. This allows the
homeowners to plant as they wish but also means they are
responsible for the yard's maintenance and care. The owners
want a patio instead of the existing lawn since it makes the
space more usable. Even though the condominium associa-
tion would take care of mowing the lawn, the owners prefer
the convenience of a hardscaped area.*

The Plan

Assessing the Design Options

Because the front yard is the only yard, it must meet all of the couple's
entertaining and gardening needs. This is not a large space, but it offers many
opportunities for design, albeit on a smaller scale than most yards. I suggested
that the couple look at the size of their lot as an advantage: costs are lower as
smaller amounts of hardscaping materials and plants are required, the work
will go quickly because there's less work to do and the final plan will yield a
landscape that requires very little upkeep.

A sidewalk leads directly from the yard's entrance to the front door and is set
off to one side, creating some visual interest. A planting bed will run between
the sidewalk and the fence at the narrowest side of the yard, leaving room for
a circular patio. This shape will make efficient use of the limited space and,
again, provide visual interest. The patio should be large enough to accommodate a small table and at least two chairs. A good-sized planting bed will
surround the patio, generously widening at two corners. To bring some visual
relief to the tall fence, an arbour will be installed over the gate and stained to
match. A cantilevered fireplace has a handy storage shed built in front of it,
and the shed's access should not be blocked with plants. Instead, a few attractive stepping stones will make getting in and out easy.

Landscape Tip

Before you plan a condominium garden, have a thorough understanding of the bylaws and regulations pertaining to your complex's outdoor spaces. Patios, paths, plants and even containers like windowboxes may be addressed in an effort to keep the architectural integrity of the condominium community.

Completed elevation

Postage Stamp Paradise

Once the patio has been installed and the planting beds have been filled with good soil, the plants can be chosen. During the summer, most of the yard will be in full sun, except for the space close to the residence, which will be in the shade during the heat of the day.

A 'Rosy O'Grady' clematis will frame the gate and welcome guests. It can be trained along the fence to soften its mass. If the fence needs to be painted or replaced, the clematis should survive being cut back.

Because even a small tree would overwhelm this space, a wiser decision is to plant a tree-form shrub. The 'Diabolo' ninebark is a striking specimen with dark leaves, white flowers and peeling bark, so I've positioned it to provide a focal point. 'Dream Weaver' ornamental crabapple is a small beauty that is very striking in spring when it's covered in blossoms. Evergreens are always nice in a garden because they provide a year-round presence, and they are low-maintenance choices that won't grow too quickly. I've chosen to add a 'Columnar Scotch' pine, a nest spruce and a hardy rhododendron to the space. The soil nearest the foundation stays damp most of the time, and this spot is shady. Rayflowers and bugbane will thrive in these conditions and provide height, interesting foliage and attractive blooms. An assortment of appropriately sized shrubs and perennials fill out the spaces between. The last step is to mulch the planting areas for a seamless appearance.

When the design is completed, the garden will provide a pleasant place for the homeowners to sit with cool drinks and have a chat at the end of a workday.

Even a tiny condominium yard can contain a seating area and room to grow a few plants.

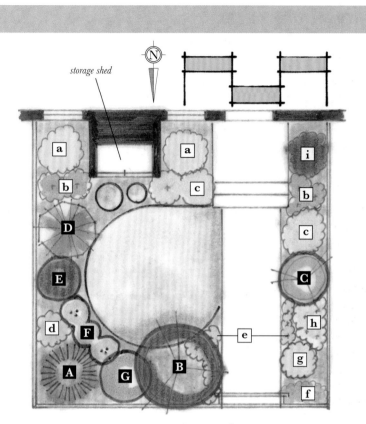

storage shed

Trees

A Pine 'Columnar Scotch'
Pinus sylvestris 'Fastigiata' .....(1)

B Ninebark 'Diabolo'
Physocarpus opulifolius
(tree form) ....(1)

C Ornamental Crabapple
'Dream Weaver'
Malus x pumila ....(1)

Shrubs

D Nest Spruce
Picea abies 'Nidiformis' ....(1)

E Barberry 'Rose Glow'
Berberis thunbergii
var. *atropurpurea* ....(1)

F Spirea 'Flaming Elf'
Spiraea japonica ....(3)

G Rhododendron 'Pohjola's Daughter'
Rhododendron ....(1)

Perennials

a Rayflower 'The Rocket'
Ligularia ....(2)

b Solomon's seal
Polygonatum ....(2) + (3)

c Hosta *Hosta* ....(2) + (1)

d Blue Oat Grass
Helictotrichon sempervirens .....(1)

e Creeping Speedwell
Veronica oltensis ....(5) + (3)

f Big Petal Clematis 'Rosy O'Grady'
Clematis macropetala ....(1)

g Daylily *Hemerocallis* ....(1)

h Martagon Lily
Lilium martagon ....(5)

i Purple Bugbane *Actaea simplex*
(syn. *Cimicifuga*) ....(1)

Simplicity

Tiny townhome garden, southern exposure

**Wish List: an attractive entrance
and low-maintenance plants.**

*One of the reasons the homeowners purchased their con-
dominium is that they are not very interested in gardening.
There is a patio, a small tree and a few shrubs to care for at
the back of their unit so they want their front entrance to be as
low maintenance as possible but to still make an impression.*

The Plan

Assessing the Design Options

Because the size and shape of the beds and a
'Showy' mountain ash are predetermined elements
that the developer installed, the homeowners need
only to decide what to plant in the two beds flanking the front steps. This area receives full sun and
because of its proximity to the building, is sheltered
from rain. It would be nice if the plant's chosen for
these tiny beds had more than one-season interest.
If in the future the owners would like change the
look of the front a little, they can add a hanging
basket from the eaves or place large containers on
either side of the garage door.

Completed elevation

Landscape Tip

Hanging baskets and containers are a great
low-maintenance way to enjoy gardening.
Choose vessels that hold enough soil to not only
support the plants but also to retain enough
water to prevent the container from drying out
too quickly. Use a slow-release fertilizer when
you plant the pots and you won't need to worry
about fertilizing again for the season. If you
go a step further and choose annuals that are
heat and drought tolerant, you may not need to
water as often—but be sure to check!

Simplicity

I suggested planting feather reed grass at the back of the beds. This perennial grass grows very tall and will create a strong vertical line in the small space. It will also provide year-round interest if it is not cut back in the fall. The addition of coralbells in front of the grass will provide a nice shot of colour through most of the growing season. Both plants I've selected are drought tolerant and low maintenance once established.

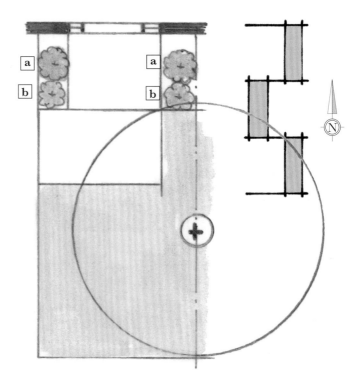

Perennials

a Feather Reed Grass 'Karl Foerster'
  Calamagrostis x *acutiflora*.......(2)

b Coralbells 'Brandon Pink'
  Heuchera sanguinea..................(2)

Country Living

Large acreage property, potential for brush fires, southern exposure

Wish List: visual impact from a distance,
"fire smart" plants and water conservation.

The homeowners have made a fantastic start to landscaping their property. A great windbreak is planted on the north-west side of the property. It consists of willows planted on the outer edge (the side exposed to the prevailing wind) and spruce on the leeward side. Their driveway has a gentle yet well-defined curve with a teardrop-shaped island bed at the centre that allows for an easy turnaround in front of the house. The row of 'Thunderchild' crabapples along the drive-way is nicely spaced, and the foliage colour and rich pink of the blossoms complement the plum-coloured front door. The owners would now like to create appeal from the road and an attractive view from their porch.

Landscape Tip

Collecting runoff from a roof and reserving it for times when there is little rain can make a huge dif-ference both to your plants and to your pocketbook, so I recommend placing a rain barrel under every downspout. They fill quickly, so always direct overflow away from foundations.

The Plan

Assessing the Design Options

Before I could come up with a design and select plants, the owners and I needed to address some issues specific to acreage living. With less-than-average annual precipitation and hot summers becoming the norm, forest and brush fires are all too common. One recommended approach to reduce the risk of a fire is to break landscapes into three zones. The first zone is within 10m of the home and should be kept free of easily combustible material. The second zone extends another 30m. In this zone, the vegetation must be thinned and cleared of readily combustible, dead and dry material—fuel. The third zone extends another 30m and beyond and is often, as in this case, out of the control of the homeowner.

Mulch can help retain soil moisture and suppress weeds, but certain types can pose a fire hazard. Rock mulch is not flammable but would be prohibitively expensive for this design. Cocoa shells have a very low flammability rating but are equally expensive, so I recommended pine bark nuggets with a particle size of 1.25 to 5cm. They have a low flammability rating and fit the budget. After consulting "Fire Smart" websites, I was dismayed to read that evergreens contain extremely flammable resins and, therefore, should be removed if they are closer than 20 to 30m from a house.

The design was a challenge, but even with many of my favourite plant choices gone, the owners and I were very pleased with the final plant selection and layout.

Stage Three elevation

Country Living—Stage One

I suggested beginning with the plantings in the teardrop-shaped bed since it is the most prominent feature of the yard. Planting a half-circle-shaped cotoneaster hedge that mirrors the outside curve of the bulbous side of the teardrop-shaped bed will visually complete the circle at that end. Inside the circle, a 'Bailey Compact' maple and some 'Charles Joly' lilacs will create a nice backdrop for the other plantings. 'Purple Leaf' sandcherries will complement the colour of the crabapples lining the driveway. The pink tones will continue in this bed with the additions of 'Pink Beauty' potentillas and extremely hardy and fragrant 'Hansa' roses. The grey-green foliage of 'Miniglobe' honeysuckles will provide nice contrast to the glossy-green leaves of the Hansas. On the other side of the cotoneaster hedge, plantings of lilacs, roses and honeysuckles will be repeated. A single red leaf rose and a group of 'Goldstar' potentillas will also be added. Toward the narrow end of the teardrop are a group of daylilies. Because they are being planted en masse, I suggest choosing varieties that flower at different times. This will lengthen their bloom period and create interest throughout the growing season. The stonecrop in this bed will be extremely easy to propagate from small cuttings, so just a few will need to be purchased. To lessen expenses, blue flax may be seeded directly into the garden. Once the perennials spread out, they will form a colourful groundcover.

The completion of this part of the garden will create some interest from the roadway and a nice view from the deck and the interior of the home.

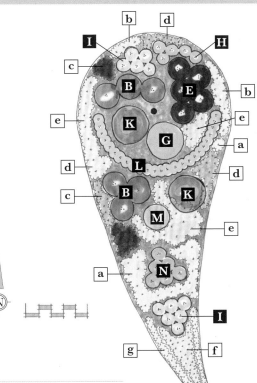

Shrubs

B Rose 'Hansa'
   Rosa .... (3) + (3)

E Sandcherry 'Purple Leaf'
   Prunus x *cistena* .... (5)

G Maple 'Bailey Compact'
   Acer tataricum
   ssp. *ginnala* .... (1)

H Potentilla 'Pink Beauty'
   Potentilla fruticosa .... (5)

I Miniglobe Honeysuckle
   Lonicera x
   xylosteoides .... (5) + (6)

K Lilac 'Charles Joly'
   Syringa vulgaris .... (1) + (1)

L Cotoneaster 'Hedge/Peking'
   Cotoneaster acutifolius .... (15)

M Red Leaf Rose *Rosa glauca* .... (1)

N Potentilla 'Goldstar'
   Potentilla fruticosa .... (6)

Perennials

a Daylily *Hemerocallis* .... (1) + (16)

b Snow-in-Summer *Cerastium*
   tomentosum .... (3) + (7)

c Peony *Paeonia* .... (3) + (3)

d Heartleaf Bergenia
   Bergenia cordifolia .... (7) + (9)

e Bigroot Cranesbill *Geranium*
   macrorrhizum ..... (4) + (14) + (10)

f Perennial Blue Flax
   Linum perenne .... (26)

g Russian Stonecrop
   Sedum kamtschaticum .... (28)

Country Living—Stage Two

This stage of the design focuses on the creation of two foundation plantings. The west bed features a 'Dreamweaver' crabapple that will add a striking vertical touch by the front steps. This crabapple is related to the Thunderchild crabapples along the drive and is extremely narrow in form. A fragrant Miss Kim lilac, a Hansa rose and a group of 'Tor' spireas round out the shrubs in this planting. Tor spirea is a native species with white flowers in the summer and intense long-lasting fall colour. I've suggested planting a few snow-in-summer to cover the ground beneath the shrubs.

On the east side, a bed extends out to the driveway and wraps around the side of the house. This bed echoes the others in some of its plant choices. Bailey Compact maple, Purple Leaf sandcherry, Pink Beauty potentilla and Hansa rose make another appearance, as do, daylilies, peonies, heartleaf bergenia and other perennials. Two more Miss Kim lilacs will be planted to bloom near a grouping of double flowering plums. Pavement roses front the bed and will provide lots of colour and fragrance during the summer.

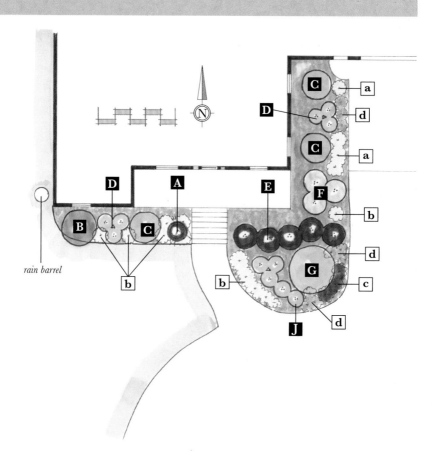

rain barrel

Trees

A Ornamental Crabapple 'Dream Weaver'
   Malus x *pumila* ....(1)

Shrubs

B Rose 'Hansa'
   Rosa ....(1)

C Lilac 'Miss Kim'
   Syringa patula ....(1) + (1) + (1)

D Spirea 'Tor'
   Spiraea betulifolia .... (3) + (3)

E Sandcherry 'Purple Leaf'
   Prunus x *cistena* ....(5)

F Double Flowering Plum
   Prunus triloba var. *multiplex* ....(3)

G Maple 'Bailey Compact'
   Acer tataricum
   ssp. *ginnala* ....(1)

J Pavement Roses
   Rosa ....(5)

Perennials

a Daylily
   Hemerocallis ....(3) + (1)

b Snow-in-Summer
   Cerastium tomentosum ....
   ....(1) + (1) + (5) + (7) + (1)

c Peony *Paeonia* .... (3) + (3) + (5)

d Heartleaf Bergenia *Bergenia*
   cordifolia .... (3) + (3) + (3)

Country Living—Stage Three

The last stage of the design focuses on creating an island bed that will provide balance to the landscape on the east side of the yard.

Here I have used repetition once more to unify the beds. A group of Charles Joly lilacs will have a strong presence in the spring, and the blooms of the redleaf rose and Pink Beauty potentillas will carry the bed through the summer. A variety of daylilies and a grouping of heartleaf bergenia will complete this bed.

It's important to note that the homeowners certainly have the space to expand this bed, and if they desired to, they could place stepping stone paths, arbours and other features into an enlarged version.

This design provides the fire break advised in my research, while still incorporating some attractive elements that will create appeal from the road.

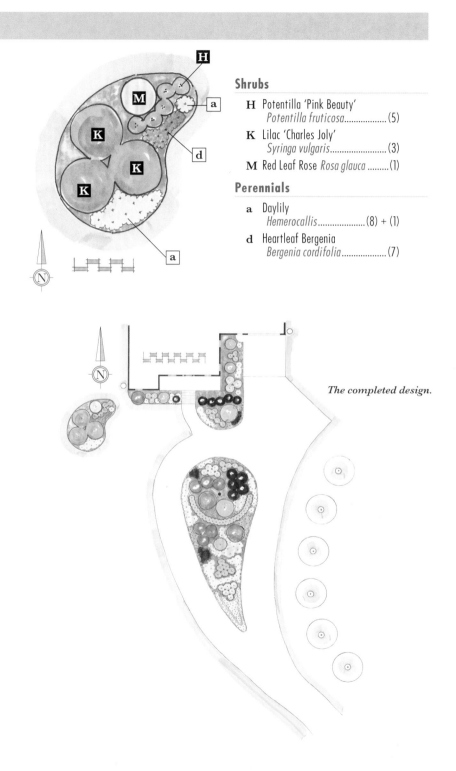

Shrubs

H Potentilla 'Pink Beauty'
Potentilla fruticosa..................(5)

K Lilac 'Charles Joly'
Syringa vulgaris.......................(3)

M Red Leaf Rose *Rosa glauca* ....(1)

Perennials

a Daylily
Hemerocallis...................(8) + (1)

d Heartleaf Bergenia
Bergenia cordifolia..................(7)

The completed design.

Simple Lines

Small house, neighbour's fence is too prominent, northern exposure

Wish List: a simple design, plants in scale with the house, bird-friendly yard and less lawn to mow.

The owners of this home are empty-nesters who purchased this small bungalow to better suit their needs. They find the neighbours' tall wooden fence quite imposing and would like to de-emphasize it. They are interested in birds but not in a lot of yard maintenance. They are willing to landscape the yard themselves but wish to handle it in manageable stages. Both owners were keen gardeners in their former home so they understand the importance of building up the soil in this yard to support the growth of plants.

The Plan

Assessing the Design Options

The homeowners and I agreed that the layout needed to be simple and in keeping with the modest design of the house. Creating planting beds with easy curves accomplishes this objective and makes mowing the lawn a snap. To further reduce the amount of lawn care and irrigation, I recommended removing the strip planted along the driveway and replacing it with ground-covering junipers.

The fence can easily be screened with a few strategically placed plants, but before planting begins, the owners will properly prepare the site by removing a sufficient amount of subsoil to allow for 45cm of new topsoil to be added to the planting areas for both stages. The addition of a birdbath near the window, along with the plants I've selected, will allow the homeowners to birdwatch discretely from indoors.

Stage Two elevation

Landscape Tip

There is nothing wrong with using straight lines to create your planting beds. Often, the architecture of a house demands them. Just ensure that the beds are broad enough to accommodate the width of the plants inside.

Simple Lines—Stage One

The first stage involves the creation of a gently curving foundation bed that is bordered by the neighbours' fence.

Planting a 'Techny' cedar and a 'Silver & Gold' dogwood along the fence will, in time, hide the fence and frame the house. Both the tree and the shrub will provide good perching sites. The dogwood will produce berries for the birds to eat, and during the winter months, will look particularly attractive when its bare yellow branches stand out against both the cedar and a nest spruce. I've also chosen to plant 'Tor' spireas in the shady spot under the front window. It's a shade-tolerant variety that will flower there, although not as much as it would in full sun. Best of all, Tor is low enough not to obscure the view of the bird bath from the front window. Throughout the bed, there will be a variety of hardy, low-maintenance perennials that will attract birds and butterflies to the garden.

Dressing the front step with a large container of shade-tolerant annuals, such as begonia, coleus, perilla and asparagus fern, will provide that last little punch needed at the front door.

Planting 'Blueberry Delight' junipers to replace the strip of grass along the driveway will add interesting colour, and their 'berries' (which actually are modified cones) will provide another source of food for birds.

The result at this stage of the design is an inviting-looking home situated within a cozy garden.

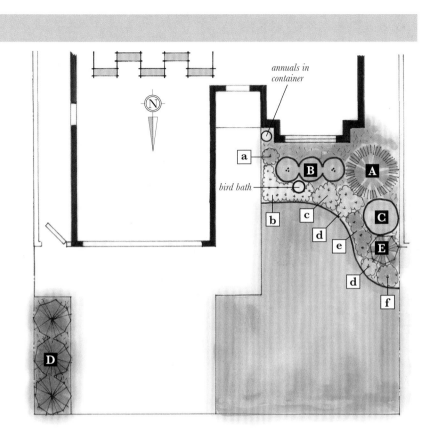

annuals in container

bird bath

Trees

A Cedar 'Techny' (Mission)
Thuja occidentalis ....(1)

Shrubs

B Spirea 'Tor'
Spiraea betulifolia ....(3)

C Dogwood 'Silver & Gold'
Cornus sericea ....(1)

D Juniper 'Blueberry Delight'
*Juniperus communis
depressa 'Amidak'* ....(3)

E Nest Spruce
Picea abies 'Nidiformis' ....(1)

Perennials

a Goat's Beard 'Kneiffii'
Aruncus dioicus ....(1)

b Auricula Primrose
Primula auricula .... (11)

c Hosta
Hosta ....(3)

d Heartleaf Bergenia
Bergenia cordifolia ....(3)

e Fernleaf Bleeding Heart
Dicentra formosa ....(3)

f Peony
Paeonia ....(1)

Simple Lines—Stage Two

The second stage of this design extends the foundation bed, modifying it to a U-shape so that it runs down the property line and along the public sidewalk. This enlarged bed will further reduce the amount of lawn.

A 'Showy' mountain ash is a good choice for a small lot and is lovely to look at year round. During winter months, flocks of hungry waxwings will come to feed on its berries. I have placed it at the front of the bed. Combining the differing foliage colours of 'Sunsation' barberries and junipers will create a tapestry effect. The addition of sun-loving perennials, such as blue sage and coneflowers, will also provide some colour and textural contrast.

The completion of this stage will give this garden a comfortable sense of enclosure and privacy, using the fence to advantage, while still maintaining a welcoming atmosphere.

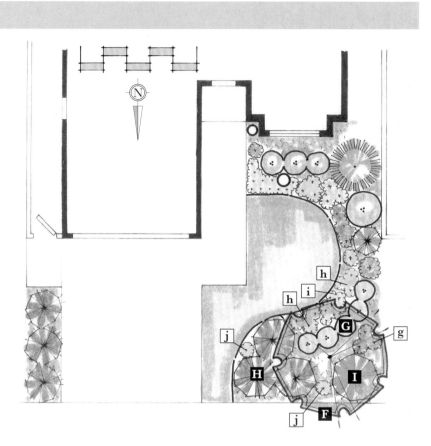

Trees

F Mountain Ash 'Showy'
    Sorbus decora ....(1)

Shrubs

G Barberry 'Sunsation' *Berberis thunbergii*
    'Monry' ....(5)

H Juniper 'Wilton's Blue Rug'
    Juniperus horizantalis
    'Wiltonii' ....(3)

I Juniper 'Mint Julep'
    Juniperus chinensis ....(1)

Perennials

g Blue Oat Grass *Helictotrichon*
    sempervirens ....(3)

h Blue Sage 'East Friesland'
    Salvia nemorosa ....(3) + (3)

j Coneflower 'Kim's Knee High'
    Echinacea ....(8)

k Lady's Mantle
    Alchemilla mollis ....(1) + (1)

Taking It Easy

Two storey home on a pie-shaped lot,
prominent garage, southern exposure

Wish List: low-maintenance plants,
less lawn and a small front garden.

*The homeowners are a busy young family with little time
to work on their yard. However, they'd still like to begin
some of their landscaping and want to start with a variety
of low-maintenance plants. They like the look of 'Swedish
Columnar' aspens, but there are already loads of them in the
neighbourhood, so they would prefer something different.
They are aware of the high water requirements of lawns and,
therefore, would like to remove some of theirs over time.*

The Plan

Assessing the Design Options

Because the homeowners' lot is pie shaped, care
needs to be taken in the placement of the beds and
in the selection of the plants. A mistake with either
could obscure the view of the house, making the
garage door the most prominent feature.

I suggested breaking the work into two stages,
which could be further subdivided if this young
family is pressed for time.

Stage Three elevation

Landscape Tip

There are two commonly used types of mulch: inorganic (or rock based) and organic (or plant based). Inorganic mulches are best used in alpine gardens, where they are needed to keep moisture away from the crowns of the plants, and in Japanese gardens, where they are integral to the design. Organic mulches are preferred in most other gardens because they improve the soil and are economical. Organic mulches vary in particle size from compost (more of a top-dressing than a mulch) to bark chunks. The size chosen depends on the amount of attractiveness that is desired. If appearance is not a concern, you may opt for arborist's chips, which can often be obtained free of charge. If appearance is important, cocoa bean hulls or dyed wood chips can be used. Organic mulches decompose over time and need to be topped up periodically.

Taking It Easy—Stage One

The most logical place to begin landscaping the yard is with a foundation bed that will anchor this tall home to its surroundings.

Once the soil requirements have been met, the planting can begin. A 'Sutherland' caragana is a great alternative to the columnar aspens that are so popular in this neighbourhood. Not only will it stand apart from the neighbours' trees, the caragana also won't be as tall, which means it should fit nicely in the tight corner by the house. Its bright-yellow flowers in late spring will look quite attractive from behind the silvery blue of the 'Table Top' juniper to be planted at its base. Lemon-yellow flowers and silvery-green foliage are the summer highlights of the 'Katherine Dykes' potentillas I've selected to place in a row along the bed's innermost curve. The potentillas will complement the yellow and blue theme that continues with blue flax and false sunflowers. Bearded iris will provide a display of spring colour right at the front door, and after a couple of years, the purple gasplant, adjacent to the irises, will flower in the early summer.

There is a narrow strip along the west side of the driveway, but because the homeowners are not yet willing to plant this area or to deal with the difficulty of mowing what would be a flimsy strip of lawn, they have decided to cover the area with a thick layer of mulch. It will be spread over the prepared topsoil to help maintain the soil structure and to inhibit weeds until the homeowners are ready to begin Stage Two.

At this point in the design, a good beginning will have been made in the presentation of the home.

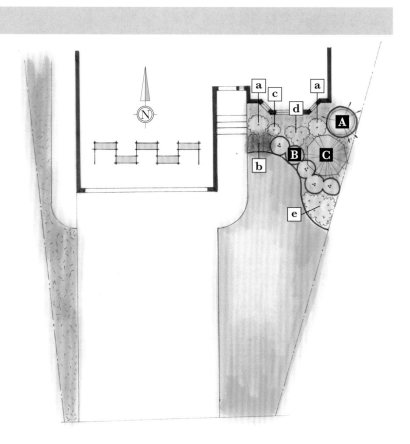

Trees

A Caragana 'Sutherland'
Caragana arborescens................(1)

Shrubs

B Potentilla 'Katherine Dykes'
Potentilla fruticosa..................(5)

C Juniper 'Table Top'
Juniperus scopulorum................(1)

Perennials

a False Sunflower
Heliopsis helianthoides ....(2)

b Bearded Iris
Iris germanica............................(5)

c Purple Gas Plant
Dictamnus albus v.
purpureus ....(1)

d Feather Reed Grass 'Overdam'
Calamagrostis x *acutiflora*......(3)

e Perennial Blue Flax
Linum perenne............................(5)

Taking It Easy—Stage Two

The next stage of this low-maintenance plan starts with the narrow strip along the driveway. The owners will remove the mulch, saving it on a tarp to be redistributed once the bed is planted.

To tie this narrow bed to the existing foundation plantings, the homeowners and I have chosen to plant another Sutherland caragana and one Katherine Dykes potentilla. Because this bed extends to the end of the driveway, they will have to be careful not to crush the potentilla with the snow they shovel from the drive, but the perennials we've selected will not be affected. This long bed will be quite a colourful feature with an interesting mix of plants.

Next, the foundation bed will be extended to reach further along the property's eastern edge. The elongated bed will accommodate a 'Thunderchild' crabapple. It is a stunning tree while in bloom, and its rich foliage colour maintains the tree's appeal through till fall. Like the caragana planted in Stage One, this crabapple is not a particularly tall tree. During winter months, its dark bark will stand out against the light colour of the house. The summer flowers of 'Neon Flash' spirea will echo the spring blossoms of the crabapple. Bookending this side of the bed with bearded irises will link this planting to the one by the front door. With the addition of a rich burgundy-coloured ground cover sedum, such as the variety 'Voodoo,' the front garden will look relatively complete.

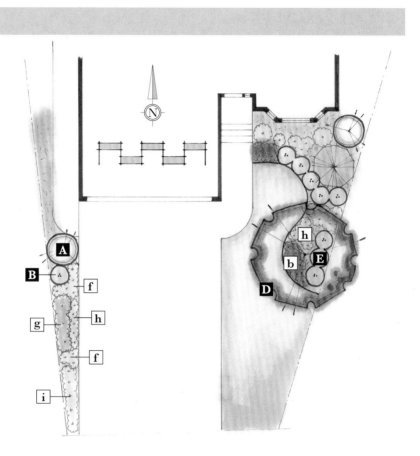

Trees

A Caragana 'Sutherland'
Caragana arborescens .... (1)

D Ornamental Crabapple 'Thunderchild'
Malus x pumila .... (1)

Shrubs

B Potentilla 'Katherine Dykes'
Potentilla fruticosa .... (1)

E Spirea 'Neon Flash'
Spiraea japonica .... (3)

Perennials

b Bearded Iris
Iris germanica .... (7)

f Blue Fescue 'Elijah Blue'
Festuca glauca .... (5) + (3)

g Peony *Paeonia* .... (3)

h Two Row Stonecrop 'Voodoo'
Sedum spurium .... (5) + (7)

i Daylily 'Hyperion'
Hemerocallis .... (5)

Taking It Easy—Stage Three

The final stage of this design requires the installation of another bed—this time down the driveway and along the public sidewalk.

The goal of the bed is to soften the expanse of the driveway and to reduce the lawn further. The plantings will be quite low, to not obscure the front door, and should be able to handle the weight of snow. A top-grafted 'Miss Kim' lilac will be the focal point of the bed. Its foliage will colour nicely in the fall, which is rare in lilacs. A 'White Bud' mugo pine will also be added at this stage and because it is a true dwarf, should not require pruning. The perennials I've selected are repetitions of existing ones and will help pull the look together.

Adding this new bed creates another layer in the garden, and the small swath of lawn that remains will set off the plantings nicely.

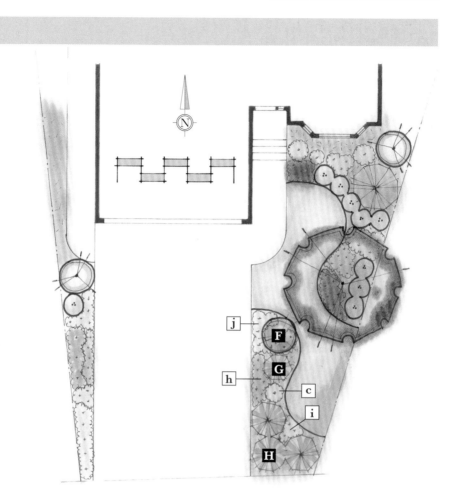

Trees

F Lilac 'Miss Kim'
  Syringa patula (tree form)........(1)

Shrubs

G Pine 'White Bud'
  Pinus mugo...............................(1)

H Juniper 'Green Carpet'
  Juniperus communis ....(3)

Perennials

c Purple Gas Plant *Dictamnus*
  albus v. *purpureus* ....(1)

h Two Row Stonecrop 'Voodoo'
  Sedum spurium ....(7)

i Daylily 'Hyperion'
  Hemerocallis.............................(3)

j Greyleaf Cranesbill 'Ballerina'
  Geranium cinereum...................(7)

Correcting Past Mistakes

Wide path to front door under a portico,
split-level with attached garage, northern exposure

Wish List: removal of spruce tree,
a pretty garden
and a cool place to sit in summer.

*The homeowners have lived in the house for a number of
years and feel that their front garden is tired looking. "Way
back when," they planted a large spruce tree along the driveway, with the idea of creating privacy, but because it eventually encroached onto the drive and sidewalk, it was limbed
up. The result is a large unattractive area beneath the tree
where little will grow and a lawn that can't compete with the
tree's moisture needs. Aside from having a tree service cut
down the spruce and grind out the stump, the homeowners
are willing to do the rest of the landscaping themselves. The
new garden must be pretty, with lots of colour.*

Stage Two elevation

The Plan

Assessing the Design Options

The home's portico (the large overhang above the entrance to the house) provides a nicely sheltered path to the front door and a strong sense of enclosure. One design option was to plant along this path, but the homeowners and I worried that it might change the space from enclosed to claustrophobic. We decided instead to go with a planting that will start at the home's front door, eventually wrap around the perimeter of the yard and terminate approximately in line with the end of the portico's roof. This plan will create clear access to the driveway and path, and the plantings will engage the attention of people walking up to the door. The garden will provide an attractive view from the interior of the house and the owners can use the space beneath the portico as a sitting area.

Landscape Tip

It's tempting to plant too close to driveways and sidewalks. Close spacing may look great when plants are young, but cute 'Calgary Carpet' junipers planted in a 60cm strip along a driveway will eventually spread to more than three times that width. The plants then require shearing, which ruins their natural shape. No wonder people often find gardening frustrating.

Correcting Past Mistakes—Stage One

Three beds will be installed in this first stage of landscaping, beginning with the foundation bed.

Most evergreens wouldn't fair well under the front window, but the 'Taunton's Spreading' yews will tolerate the shade, and the variegated leaves of the *Pulmonaria*—a tough shade perennial—will create a bright contrast against the yews' dark-green foliage. The hardy nannyberry will also grow in shady conditions, making it ideal for the west corner of the house. It will also take on the task of screening the homeowners' entrance from that of their neighbours. A 'Coppertina' ninebark and 'Goldmound' spireas along the property's edge will be striking, and a planting of 'Golden Tiara' hostas will pick up the foliage colour of the spireas. A nest spruce is always a fine addition to a shrub bed and will create a background for the coralbells. I've also selected a 'Brunette' bug-bane for this planting bed. Its foliage will echo that of the ninebark, and in the late summer, its fragrant white flower spikes will be a lovely greeting for visitors.

A fast-growing 'Prairie Splendor' maple will be planted in an island bed located near the front of the yard. This shade tree's maroon foliage will create eye-catching contrast with the other trees in the neighbourhood. Four large boulders will be placed around this tree. 'Magic Carpet' spireas continue the colour theme from the foundation bed. Other plantings will be repeated here to create unity. For example, a grouping of blue fescue with a solitary coralbell was selected to correspond to the plantings beside the nest spruce.

Finally, a bed will be created along the driveway. More Goldmound spireas will be planted next to a tree form 'Kesselring' dogwood, which will create a vertical accent that is in scale with the space. A row of coralbells will provide a tidy swath of colour in the summer, and at the end of the driveway, a grouping of bergenias will be planted to create a visual link to those in the island bed.

At this point, the front garden will take on the attractive appearance the owners desired.

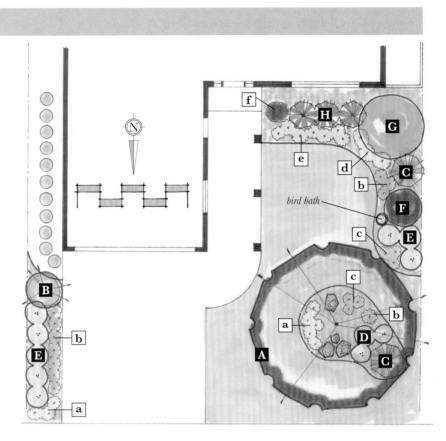

Trees

A Maple 'Prairie Splendor'
    Acer platanoides.......................(1)

B Dogwood 'Kesselring'
    Cornus alba 'Kesselringii'
    (Tree form) ....(1)

Shrubs

C Nest Spruce *Picea abies*
    'Nidiformis' ....(1) + (1)

D Spirea 'Magic Carpet'
    Spiraea japonica.......................(3)

E Spirea 'Goldmound'
    Spiraea japonica.............(5) + (3)

F Ninebark 'Coppertina' *Physocarpus
    opulifolius* 'Mindia' ....(1)

G Nannyberry
    Viburnum lentago......................(1)

H Yew 'Taunton's Spreading'
    Taxus x media 'Tauntonii' ....(3)

Perennials

a Heartleaf Bergenia
    Bergenia cordifolia.........(5) + (3)

b Coralbells
    Heuchera ....(7) + (3) + (1)

c Blue Fescue
    Festuca glauca ....(3) + (3)

d Hosta 'Golden Tiara' *Hosta*........(3)

e Bethlehem Sage 'Argentea'
    Pulmonaria saccharata ....(7)

f Bugbane 'Brunette'
    Actaea simplex ....(1)

Correcting Past Mistakes—Stage Two

This stage may be implemented at any time the homeowners decide they want to expand their front garden. It really only involves linking the foundation bed to the island bed and expanding the northern edge of the island bed.

The newly created planting space between the foundation bed and the island bed will make an excellent home for a cutleaf stephanandra, and adding a 'Soongoricus' cotoneaster along the perimeter of the link will create an even stronger sense of privacy in the front garden. It will be covered with small white flowers in the spring and with brightly coloured red fruit later in the season. It will not colour as nicely in the fall as a 'Hedge' cotoneaster will, but its attractiveness throughout the summer will more than make up for that shortcoming. In the front portion of the expanded island bed, 'Wilton's Blue Rug' junipers will make an excellent ground cover, and when combined with a 'Whitebud' mugo pine, will eventually fill the area. Bold-looking ornamental grasses and divided perennials from other plantings in the yard can be used to fill any empty spaces.

With the expansion of the beds completed, the front yard will have an even more welcoming feeling.

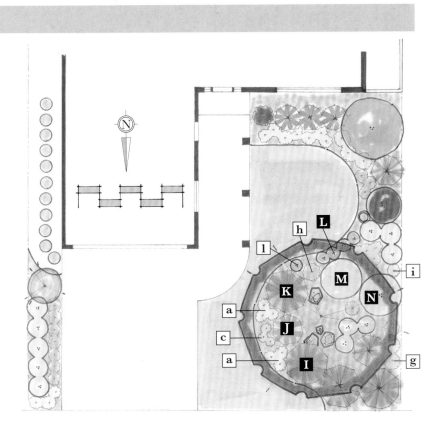

Shrubs

I Juniper 'Youngstown' (Andorra)
Juniperus horizontalis
'Andorra' .... (3)

J Pine 'White Bud'
Pinus mugo .... (1)

K Juniper 'Wilton's Blue Rug'
Juniperus horizantalis
'Wiltonii' .... (1)

L Potentilla 'Nuuk'
Potentilla tridentata .... (5)

M Cutleaf Stephanandra
Stephanandra incisa 'Crispa' .... (1)

N Cotoneaster 'Soongoricus' *Cotoneaster racemiflorus* var. *soongoricus* ... (1)

Perennials

a Heartleaf Bergenia *Bergenia cordifolia* .... (3) + (3)

c Blue Fescue
Festuca glauca .... (3) + (3)

g Blue Oat Grass *Helictotrichon sempervirens* .... (3)

h Peony *Paeonia* .... (1)

l Feather Reed Grass 'Overdam'
Calamagrostis x *acutiflora* .... (1)

Out With The Old

Overgrown plants, pie-shaped lot,
tight access, eastern exposure

Wish List: a fresh start, room to maneuver
and a home for a special tree seedling.

*The homeowners are a young family who has purchased a
30-year-old home. The original landscaping consisted of a
weeping birch and a blue spruce, planted too close together.
The birch suffered a lot of drought damage and had to be
removed. The remaining lopsided spruce, bare of branches
where the birch had encroached on it, was removed, as was
a scale-riddled cotoneaster hedge along the garage side of the
driveway. The family plans to live in this house for a long
time so are willing to invest some time in renovating the
front yard. They'd like the design to create a view from the
house and incorporate room for the Arbor Day tree seedling
their five year old will receive in Grade 1.*

Stage Two elevation

The Plan

Assessing the Design Options

With all the family activities that involve driving the kids to and from places, it makes sense to allow for a comfortable staging area. Installing a generous pathway on each side of the driveway will create that space, and providing a pleasant landscaped view from the veranda will encourage the family to make use of this sheltered area. The planting bed in front of the living room will need to be quite large to be enjoyed from both the street and from the interior of the house, so the addition of a small planting area next to the garage will help balance out the yard. The last consideration is a spot for the Arbor Day tree. Giving the seedling plenty of space to grow will help it become a symmetrical specimen that hopefully won't meet the same fate as the lot's birch and spruce.

Landscape Tip

Dividing plants is an excellent way to stretch gardening dollars and is not difficult—just choose the appropriate dividing method for the type of plant you are working with.

• Large perennials can be divided using a sharp spade to split the plant in two.

• Small perennials can be divided using a sharp knife to divide the root in two or three pieces.
  Make sure each piece has a growing point and some roots.
• Some perennials can be easily pulled apart with your hands. Ensure that each set of leaves has its own stems and roots.

Out With The Old—Stage One

After the pathways are installed, work can begin on the two beds that make up this stage of the design.

Starting on the bed in front of the home, a 'Brandon' cedar will provide a strong vertical element at the corner of the house, and an arc-shaped planting of 'Abbottswood' potentillas and a group of 'Blue Muffin' arrowwoods will create a sense of enclosure. For a shade tree, I've recommended a 'Ventura' maple. It's relatively small and won't compete with the Arbor Day tree as they grow toward each other.

'Calgary Carpet' junipers and a 'Tannenbaum' dwarf pine will line the path to the front door, and a grouping of 'Lime Glow' junipers will deliver a burst of colour. Tucked between the shrubs and the house will be a pocket garden of shade-tolerant perennials.

The Arbor Day tree is to be planted in its own circular bed, which can be enlarged as the tree widens. The homeowners can add annuals if they choose.

To balance out the other side of the yard, a 'Swedish Columnar' aspen will be planted along the driveway. An arbour over the gate will support 'Blue Bird' clematis, and the clematis' roots will be shaded by perennials.

At this stage of the design, the layout will provide a solid framework to showcase the home.

Trees

A Maple 'Ventura'
Acer tataricum ssp. *ginnala* .....(1)

B Aspen 'Swedish Columnar'
Populus tremula 'Erecta' ....(1)

C Child's Arbor Day Tree ....(1)

D Cedar 'Brandon'
Thuja occidentalis ....(1)

Shrubs

E Potentilla 'Abbotswood'
Potentilla fruticosa.................(5)

F Arrowwood 'Blue Muffin'
Viburnum dentatum
'Christom' ....(3)

G Juniper 'Calgary Carpet'
Juniperus sabina 'Monna'.........(3)

H Spruce 'Blue Nest'
Picea mariana 'Ericoides' ....(1)

I Pine 'Tannenbaum'
Pinus mugo ....(1)

J Juniper 'Lime Glow'
Juniperus horizontalis..............(2)

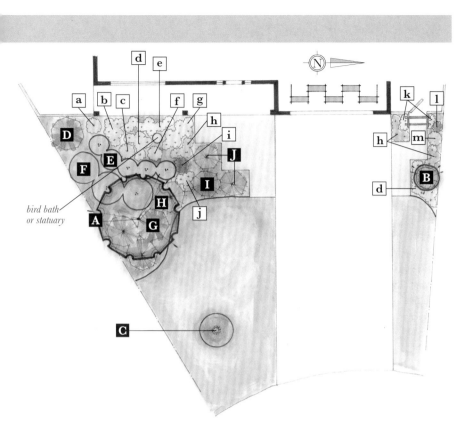

bird bath
or statuary

Perennials

a Goldleaf Bleeding Heart
'Goldheart' *Dicentra
spectabilis* ....(1)

b Coralbells 'Chocolate Ruffles'
Heuchera ....(5)

c Hosta 'Sum & Substance'
Hosta...(1)

d Blue Fumitory 'China Blue'
Corydalis flexuosa..........(5) + (7)

e Bethlehem Sage 'Argentea'
Pulmonaria saccharata ....(7)

f Rayflower 'The Rocket'
Ligularia ....(1)

g Pacific Bleeding Heart 'King of Hearts'
Dicentra ....(7)

h Heartleaf Bergenia *Bergenia
cordifolia* ....(3) + (3) + (3)

i Siberian Iris 'Caesar's Brother'
Iris sibirica ....(1)

j Feather Reed Grass 'Overdam'
Calamagrostis x *acutiflora* ......(3)

k Big Petal Clematis 'Blue Bird'
Clematis macropetala ....(1) +(1)

l Monkshood 'Stainless Steel'
Aconitum napellus ....(1)

m Goat's Beard 'Kneiffii'
Aruncus dioicus ....(1)

Out With The Old—Stage Two

This stage of the design calls for the removal of the strip of lawn between the driveway and the property line. This bed will allow the homeowners to grow a few more plants without interfering with the driveway's function.

The strong blue-grey colour of a 'Moonglow' juniper will highlight this spot of the yard, as will the attractive leathery leaves of the 'Mohican' wayfaring tree I've selected. To relate this garden to the one on the other side, I've chosen to repeat the Abbottswood potentilla, the Lime Glow juniper and some of the other perennials. The owner can save money by dividing the existing perennials—providing they are large enough to do so.

I reminded the owners that, although they were quite keen to plant this area, they must be careful to not split any of the shrubs with the snow they remove from the driveway and pile here each winter. Placing the snow carefully around the shrubs—and keeping the kids off the snow bank—will prevent any serious damage.

When this stage is completed, the plantings will provide visual weight to the garage side of the driveway.

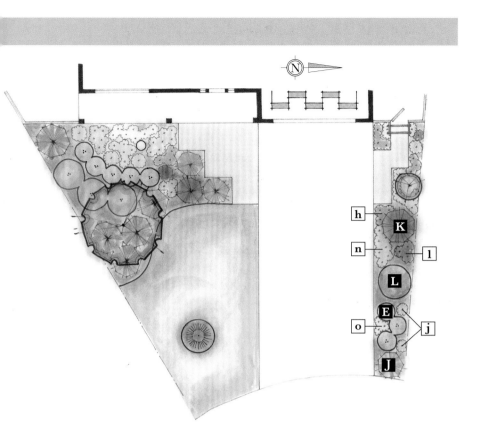

Trees

K Juniper 'Moonglow'
Juniperus scopulorum ....(1)

Shrubs

E Potentilla 'Abbotswood'
Potentilla fruticosa ....(3)

J Juniper 'Lime Glow'
Juniperus horizontalis ....(1)

L Wayfaring Tree 'Mohican'
Viburnum lantana ....(1)

Perennials

h Heartleaf Bergenia
Bergenia cordifolia ....(3)

j Feather Reed Grass 'Overdam'
Calamagrostis x acutiflora ....(2)

l Monkshood 'Stainless Steel'
Aconitum napellus ....(3)

n Daylily *Hemerocallis* ....(7)

o Blue Fescue 'Elijah Blue'
Festuca glauca ....(3)

Out With The Old—Stage Three

The final stage of this design calls for the integration of the treasured Arbor Day tree. As the tree increases in width, it will become time to unite the two beds.

I've selected a 'Coppertina' ninebark and some 'Pink Parasols' spirea to bridge the gap between the established foundation bed and the one surrounding the tree. They should grow fairly rapidly to fill any awkward space. The ninebark I've chosen is much like the 'Diabolo' variety, but its newly emerging leaves have a coppery cast. The soft-pink flowers of the spireas will show up well against the Coppertina, and their fall colour is outstanding. In the interest of unity and economy, all the perennials used in this stage will be divisions of existing ones.

The front garden is now complete. The sitting area by the entrance is fairly private, the Arbor Day tree has room to continue to grow and the plantings don't overwhelm the house. The family should be able to move easily from driveway to house and still enjoy their landscape.

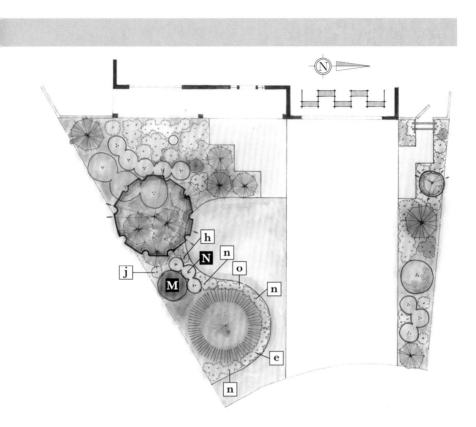

Shrubs

M Ninebark 'Coppertina' *Physocarpus opulifolius* 'Mindia' ....(1)

N Spirea 'Pink Parasols' *Spiraea fritschiana* 'Wilma' ......(3)

Perennials

e Bethlehem Sage 'Argentea' *Pulmonaria saccharata* ....(7)

h Heartleaf Bergenia *Bergenia cordifolia* ....(3)

j Feather Reed Grass 'Overdam' *Calamagrostis x acutiflora* ....(2)

n Daylily *Hemerocallis* ....(7)

o Blue Fescue 'Elijah Blue' *Festuca glauca* ....(3)

Cramped Style

Cramped walkway and entry to house,
lack of privacy, eastern exposure

Wish List: a spacious entry and walkway,
privacy, a hedge instead of a fence,
a seating area and an arbour.

*The homeowners have lived in the house for a number of
years and both enjoy gardening. Their back garden is as
planted up as possible, so they are now turning their attention to the front yard. The need to remove an aggressive and
messy poplar has given them the opportunity to start from
scratch. Neither homeowner is interested in doing any of the
hardscaping so, instead, will hire a contractor. They also
wish to do the landscaping in manageable stages to allow
themselves time to prepare the soil properly for planting.*

Landscape Tip

A thick layer of winter
mulch (chopped leaves,
pine needles and ever-
green boughs) is often
all that is needed to
help over-winter tender
herbaceous perennials.
Apply mulch after the
ground has frozen to
avoid creating a cozy
home for rodents.

Stage Two elevation

The Plan

Assessing the Design Options

One of homeowners' main objectives is to address the cramped access to their front door. Their original idea was to extend the entry and stairs by 30cm. This would allow for a bit more space by the door, but I cautioned that it wouldn't really solve the problem—the entry would remain cramped, and visitors would still need to take a step back when the front door was opened to them. The original expansion idea also fails to address the issue of the narrow path leading to the door.

A better solution is to widen the path to 1.4m (allowing visitors the option of walking side by side) and to construct a low deck across the front of the house, providing a roomier and safer entrance. By simply extending the length of the original path by 4m, better access is achieved from the driveway. As for the new deck, it will be less than 60cm from the ground and, according to my municipality's building code, won't require a railing. This means the view from the interior of the house won't be obstructed.

Privacy is also a concern because a public walkway runs along the side of the property. Originally, a fence ran to the end of the property line, but the homeowners are interested in planting a hedge in its place. Having the fence end in line with the corner of the garage and planting the hedge to run the remainder of the lot, will give the homeowners the privacy they desire.

Cramped Style—Stage One

After the new path and the deck have been completed, a 2.4m-high trellis will be installed on the the deck's north side, and an arbour will be placed at a 45 degree angle to it. This will provide extra privacy from the public walkway. An informal path of concrete slabs will then be placed to allow access to the back garden. If desired, thyme or other low-spreading perennials may be planted around the slabs to soften the look.

Two 'Polish Spirit' clematis will be planted next to the trellis and one on either side of the arbour. I chose this variety because it needs to be cut back annually and, therefore, will stay tidier looking. 'Fairy Queen' spirea, 'Overdam' feather reed grass and bergenia will cover the base of the deck, and a 'Ruby Spice' summersweet planted near the arbour will provide fragrant flowers late in the season. This foundation bed extends to include the hedge along the property line, which will be created from reliable 'Hedge/Peking' cotoneasters. These shrubs have rich, glossy summer foliage and outstanding fall colour. Cotoneasters look good even during the winter because of their dense masses of branches. The planting distance from the property line is important and should be one-half the hedge's intended spread.

A 'Harvest Gold' linden will be the shade tree. It has an excellent form, fragrant summer flowers and nice colour in the fall. It is planted fairly close to the property line, but this isn't a problem because its canopy will not be growing over a neighbour's property. In time, the linden will develop peeling bark, which will provide added interest.

The bed at the end of the lengthened path contains a light post that will be nestled among 'Blue Forest' junipers. They will add a lovely colour contrast, and their interesting growth habit will create visual appeal.

Once this stage is completed, the landscape will have a fairly finished look and the owners' most pressing concerns will have been addressed.

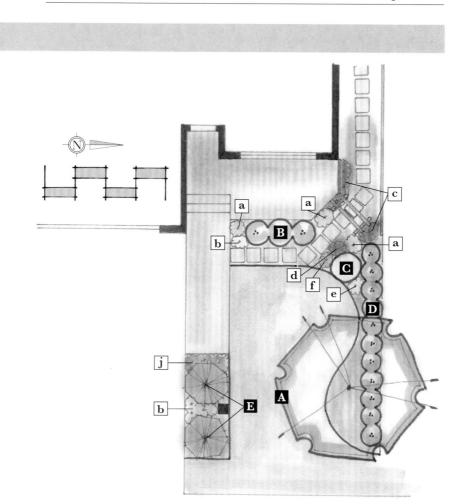

Trees

A Linden 'Harvest Gold'
   Tilia mongolica ....(1)

Shrubs

B Spirea 'Fairy Queen'
   Spiraea trilobata ....(3)

C Summersweet 'Ruby Spice'
   Clethra alnifolia ....(1)

D Cotoneaster 'Hedge/Peking'
   Cotoneaster acutifolius ....(11)

E Juniper 'Blue Forest'
   Juniperus sabina ....(2)

Perennials

a Feather Reed Grass 'Overdam'
   Calamagrostis
   x acutiflora ....(1) + (1) + (1)

b Heartleaf Bergenia
   Bergenia cordifolia ....(4) + (1)

c Virgin's Bower Clematis 'Polish Spirit'
   Clematis viticella...(2) + (1) + (1)

d Liatris *Liatris spicata* ....(1)

e Daylily *Hemerocallis* ....(1)

f Coneflower *Echinacea* ....(1)

j Creeping Speedwell
   Veronica oltensis ....(4)

Cramped Style—Stage Two

This stage of the design sees the creation of one long, sinuous foundation bed that carves away more of the lawn, making room for more plants.

The plants selected have everything to do with colour and contrast. A 'Blue Arrow' juniper will pick up the colour of the Blue Forest junipers planted in Stage One and will become a strong vertical element near the entrance of the house. The yellow-green of the 'Goldmound' spirea I've chosen to add to the bed with the light post will be nicely set off by the junipers. The variegated foliage of a 'Carol Mackie' daphne, which will be planted next to the linden, will contrast well against the rich green of the hedge and also provide fragrant blossoms in the spring—a treat to anyone walking along the public path.

Peonies are reliable perennials with lovely flowers in the spring and interesting foliage throughout the summer. However, many people don't care for them because the flowers become heavy and flop over if not supported by cages. Fortunately, there are many beautiful varieties with single flowers that don't require support. Blue fescue, coralbells and creeping speedwell will also be planted to add colour and texture to the garden.

With those final additions, the garden is complete. It says 'Welcome to our door' and hints at the attractions to be found in the back garden.

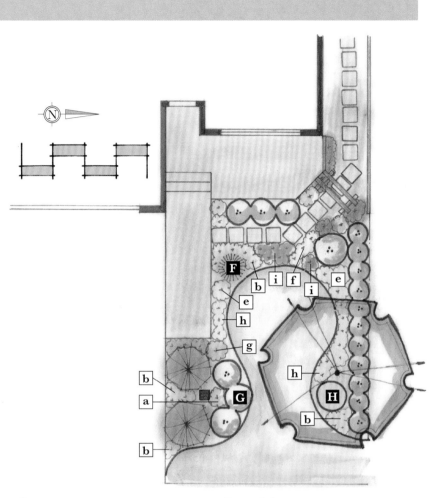

Trees

F Juniper 'Blue Arrow'
 Juniperus scopulorum .... (1)

Shrubs

G Spirea 'Goldmound'
 Spiraea japonica .... (3)

H Daphne 'Carol Mackie'
 Daphne x burkwoodii .... (1)

Perennials

a Feather Reed Grass 'Overdam'
 Calamagrostis x acutiflora .... (3)

b Heartleaf Bergenia *Bergenia
 cordifolia* .... (3) + (1) + (5)

e Daylily *Hemerocallis* .... (1) + (2)

f Coneflower *Echinacea* .... (2)

g Peony *Paeonia* .... (1)

h Blue Fescue 'Elijah Blue'
 Festuca glauca .... (6)

i Coralbells *Heuchera* .... (5) + (1)

Raising Beds— And Interests

Decided slope towards neighbour's yard, ugly skirting on veranda, view of utility box, northern exposure

**Wish List: a raised bed, privacy
and an attractive view from the veranda.**

The homeowners are a young couple who don't have any real interest in gardening but want their home to look as nice as the others on their street. They aren't sure how long they will be living in this home so want to do only what is necessary for now. One of the homeowners worked for a landscaping contractor for a couple of summers and knows he can do a good job of building the raised bed that is needed to level the planting area in front of the veranda.

Stage Three elevation

The Plan

Assessing the Design Options

When I first saw this yard, the only thing in it was a green ash the municipality planted. There is not a lot of yard to work with, but the homeowners and I agreed that there are a few interesting things that can be accomplished, starting with a raised bed. There are a number of 45 degree angles particular to both the house and the trim around the garage door. A raised bed in front of the veranda will repeat these angles. This bed will begin at the first step along the path leading to the front door. To soften and anchor the raised bed, an additional planting bed will be created in front of it. Privacy, a hidden veranda skirt and the owners' desire to fit into the neighbourhood are all accomplished by the creation of these beds.

In the later stages of the design, I suggested that integrating the municipality's tree and framing the driveway will improve the view and—if the owners decide to move—the landscaping they've invested in will increase the resale value of the property.

Landscape Tip

A raised bed made of interlocking concrete blocks may be one of the more high priced elements in your landscape, so be certain that it is installed properly. It will need to be excavated to the proper depth and have a properly prepared base to ensure that it will be level. A raised bed that has obvious dips or gaps between the blocks will draw attention to its defects rather than to the lovely plantings within it.

Raising Beds—And Interests—Stage One

Once the beds around the veranda's base have been installed and filled with quality topsoil, a visit to the nursery for plants will be in order.

A 'Brandon' cedar planted between the homeowners' house and the neighbour's will, eventually, create some privacy. It will get lots of sun in the early part of the day, and with the downspout nearby, it shouldn't want for moisture.

Next, a planting of three 'Little Giant' cedars in the raised bed will hide the unattractive lattice skirt on the veranda that the owners dislike, and a 'Cream Cracker' dogwood will provide nice contrast to the cedars. The colour variegation of the dogwood will be repeated in the foliage of 'Patriot' hostas. With the exception of the hosta's, all of these plants will provide interest—and coverage—all year.

I've selected a 'Ventura' maple to sit near the property's edge in the ground level bed to be located in front of the raised bed. It won't be too imposing in this space, will add to the privacy of the veranda and will start to screen the utility box that sits on the corner of the neighbours' lot. The blue-green foliage of the 'New Blue Tam' junipers planted beneath the maple will be set off nicely by the lawn. The heartleaf bergenias (an evergreen perennial) planted in a group will look great early in the spring, and their colour should set off the material used to create the raised bed. Rudbeckia will provide late summer and fall colour.

The raised bed deals effectively with the grading issue, the plants will provide privacy as they grow and enough landscaping has taken place to make this home fit into its surroundings.

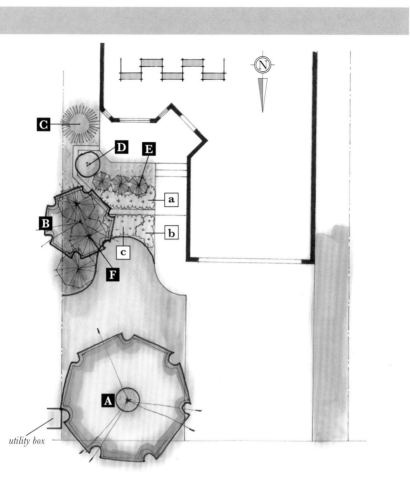

utility box

Existing Tree

A Ash 'Green'
Fraxinus pensylvanica ....(1)

Trees

B Maple 'Ventura'
Acer tataricum ssp. *ginnala* .....(1)

C Cedar 'Brandon'
Thuja occidentalis ....(1)

Shrubs

D Dogwood 'Cream Cracker'
Cornus alba ....(1)

E Cedar 'Little Giant'
Thuja occidentalis ....(3)

F Juniper 'New Blue Tam'
Juniperus sabina.........................(3)

Perennials

a Hosta 'Patriot'
Hosta..(5)

b Heartleaf Bergenia
Bergenia cordifolia...................(3)

c Black-Eyed Susan 'Goldsturm'
Rudbeckia fulgida
var. *sullivantii* ....(5)

Raising Beds—And Interests—Stage Two

At this stage of the design, the homeowners can begin to deal with the not too pretty utility box in their neighbour's yard and work toward integrating the green ash the municipality planted.

An outwardly curving bed will be created to sit in the corner of the lot extending from the tree's base, bordered by the neighbours' property and the public sidewalk. Its shape complements the foundation bed created in Stage One.

An arc of 'Nugget' ninebark will provide colour contrast in the summer, branch texture in winter and, most importantly, will hide the utility box all year. A 'Pumila' spruce and a 'Blueberry Delight' juniper will make an attractive evergreen combination, with the juniper picking up the colour of the New Blue Tam junipers I've selected for the foundation bed. The Himalayan fleece-flowers will fill in quickly, making a wonderful groundcover that also provides gorgeous fall colour similar to the maple planted in Stage One. Lastly, I suggested more heartleaf bergenias. They unify the plantings but also can perhaps be divided from Stage One's beds to save money.

Creating this planting bed around the tree on the municipally owned portion of the property will make the tree appear part of the front garden, create more privacy and hide that ugly utility box.

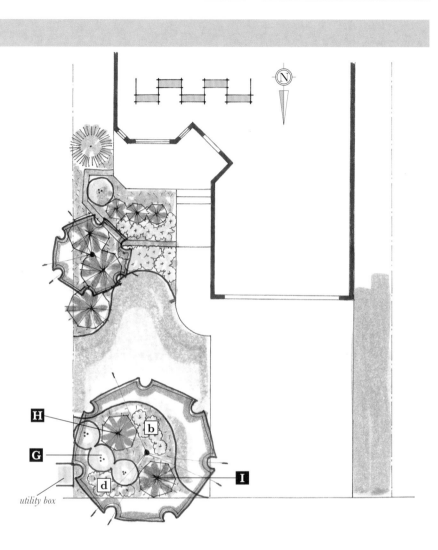

utility box

Shrubs

F Ninebark 'Nugget'
  Physocarpus opulifolius .... (3)

G Spruce 'Pumila'
  Picea abies .... (1)

H Juniper 'Blueberry Delight'
  Juniperus communis depressa
  'Amidak' .... (1)

Perennials

b Heartleaf Bergenia
  Bergenia cordifolia .... (5)

d Himalayan Fleece Flower
  'Darjeeling Red'
  Persicaria affinis .... (5)

Raising Beds—And Interests—Stage Three

In this final stage, the foundation and corner beds will be linked, creating a pretty frame for this side of the lot. To complete this landscape, one last bed will be created to replace the strip of grass along the driveway.

Joining the two beds will establish a well-defined border between the homeowners' and the neighbour's yards. I've selected 'Winnipeg Parks' roses for this area for two reasons: the flowers and foliage will provide plenty of summer colour, and the Parkland rose series, of which this rose is one, is hardy and easy to care for—a positive introduction to the world of roses. One more New Blue Tam juniper and some hostas round out this planting.

The last bed along the property's west boundary will give people something other than the driveway and the garage door to look at. Creating a short stepping stone path will allow the paper boy and letter carriers to take a shortcut from the homeowners' driveway to that of their neighbours without damaging plants. To disguise the downspout that crosses the path to the rear of the house, an arbour will be planted with 'Polish Spirit' clematis. The willows and the other plantings in this area will like the extra moisture from the roof runoff. A Blueberry Delight juniper and the repetition of a few perennials used in other plantings will complete the look and help unify both sides of the yard.

When completed, this design will give the homeowners a distinct, balanced and welcoming front garden, and—who knows?—They may just choose to stay.

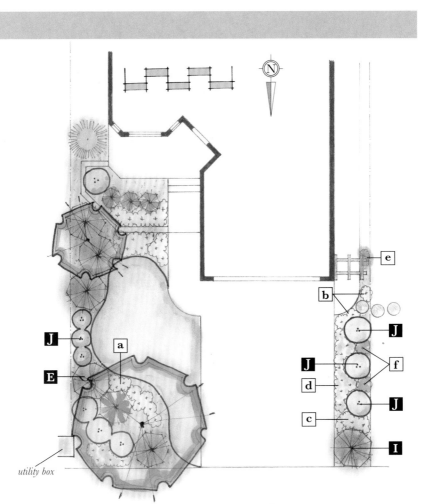

utility box

Shrubs

F Juniper 'New Blue Tam'
Juniperus sabina ....(1)

I Juniper 'Blueberry Delight'
*Juniperus communis
depressa* 'Amidak' ....(1)

J Willow 'Dwarf Arctic Blue Leaf'
Salix purpurea 'Nana' ....(3)

K Rose 'Winnipeg Parks'
Rosa ....(3)

Perennials

a Hosta 'Patriot' *Hosta* ....(3)

b Heartleaf Bergenia
Bergenia cordifolia ....(3)

c Black-Eyed Susan 'Goldsturm'
*Rudbeckia fulgida
var. sullivantii*............................(3)

d Himalayan Fleece Flower 'Darjeeling Red'
Persicaria affinis ....(8)

e Virgin's Bower Clematis 'Polish Spirit'
Clematis viticella......................(1)

f Feather Reed Grass 'Karl Foerster'
Calamagrostis x *acutiflora*........(2)

Cutting Corner Lots

Foot traffic cuts across property,
too much lawn to maintain,
southwestern exposure

Wish List: redirected foot traffic, visual
appeal from two sides and an easy-maintenance landscape.

When the homeowners bought their property a few years
ago, they realized living on a corner lot would require a bit
of extra work; however, they are now tiring of the effort. Not
only are people cutting across the corner of the lot and wear-
ing down the grass, there is a lot of grass to tend to—and not
just their own; they have two boulevard strips to care for. The
homeowners have budget considerations but know they need
a contractor to do the initial work. They are willing to spread
the project out over a couple of years.

Landscape Tip

It is a mistake to attach a trellis directly
to a structure unless you are using it as
art or to hang things from. If the trellis
is going to support a plant, you need to
have a minimum space of 5cm between
it and the struc-
ture to which
you're attaching
it. If the trellis has
legs, push them
about 15cm into
the ground and
secure the upper
portion with
brackets 15cm
from the wall
or fence.

The Plan

Assessing the Design Options

The homeowners are dealing with natural desire lines—the paths people take with no regard to the paved paths that subdivision planners have laid out. This happens most often when paved walkways are at 90 degree angles to each other, as in the case of corner lots. To correct the problem, there are two options: fight the flow, or accept it. If we chose the first option and planted a hedge up to the corner, people might walk through it until it fills in. The second option is the better one because it acknowledges that the sidewalk path is unnatural and it allows for design options that will accommodate everyone. We settled on a plan that will include a perimeter planting along the sides of the lot with a generous curve of crushed gravel to direct foot traffic along a more natural path. The path next to the driveway will be enlarged to allow for better access to vehicles and to create a direct path to the front door. Finally, a bed enclosing a semi-private seating area under an existing pergola will be created at the front of the house to reduce the amount of lawn. While the contractor is on site working on the landscape's hard elements, the homeowners will ask him to create a contoured L-shaped bed/berm that will define the lot's corner borders and to excavate the bed along the driveway, making it deep enough to accommodate 45cm of new soil.

Stage Three elevation (side view)

Cutting Corner Lots—Stage One

Once the contractor's work is complete, the owners can start on the yard, beginning with the foundation bed where old and cruelly sheared junipers will be removed and replaced with more appropriately sized 'Pumila' spruce. Feather reed grass will add a touch of drama. Highlighting the gate to the back garden will be a 'Montana Green' juniper, surrounded by blue fescue and Himalayan fleece flower.

Next, the L-shaped bed/berm will be contoured. This bed will start at ground level on all sides, eventually rising to 30cm at the highest point at the corner of the 'L.' A curve of crushed gravel, edged with decorative rock, will direct foot traffic at the corner where the public sidewalks intersect. The gravel for this path may be laid over landscape fabric.

A lodgepole pine will be planted in the corner at the bed's highest point and will become a feature for the entire street. Sedums, barberries and junipers planted nearby will provide foliage colour throughout the growing season and interest during the winter. For the end of the bed closest to the house, I proposed a 'Bur' oak for its longevity and striking winter appearance. This tree is a relatively slow grower but, in time, will shade the house nicely. A hedge of 'Fireball' burning bush centred in the bed connects the two feature trees. Day-lilies fill the space between the hedge and the public sidewalk, and on the other side, hostas and coralbells are featured.

A small planting pocket positioned at the pergola's trellised entrance, next to the garage, will be planted with a 'Henry Kelsey' rose. It will cover the trellis nicely and provide a bit of privacy for anyone seated on the new patio beneath the pergola. 'Silver Carpet' lamb's ear will grow at its base. This variety is a good choice because it doesn't flower and, therefore, won't reseed.

Another hedge of burning bush will be planted next to the driveway. These shrubs will come into their own during the fall, providing long-lasting brilliant colour. Their ridged bark also looks beautiful when exposed in winter.

With the completion of this stage of the plan, the lot's traffic and lawn maintenance issues are now solved, and views into and out from the yard are much improved.

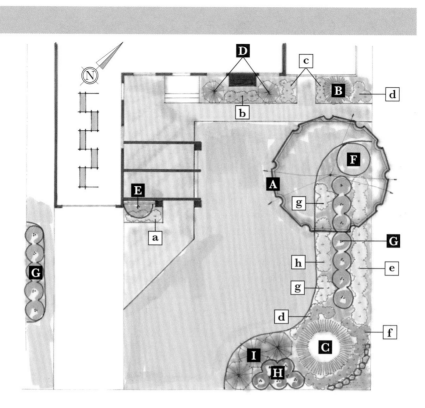

Trees

A Oak 'Bur'
Quercus macrocarpa ....(1)

B Juniper 'Montana Green'
Juniperus scopulorum ....(1)

C Lodgepole Pine
Pinus contorta var. *latifolia* ......(1)

Shrubs

D Spruce 'Pumila'
Picea abies..............................(2)

E Rose 'Henry Kelsey'
Rosa ....(1)

F Cutleaf Stephanandra
Stephanandra incisa 'Crispa' ....(1)

G Burning Bush 'Fire Ball'
Euonymus alatus.............(7) + (5)

H Barberry 'Ruby Carousel'
Berberis thunbergii var. *atropurpurea*
'Bailone'....................................(5)

I Juniper 'Blueberry Delight'
Juniperus communis depressa
'Amidak' ....(3)

Perennials

a Lamb's Ears 'Silver Carpet'
Stachys byzantina....................(3)

b Feather Reed Grass 'Karl Foerster'
Calamagrostis x acutiflora.......(3)

c Blue Fescue
Festuca glauca ....(5) + (3)

d Himalayan Fleece Flower 'Darjeeling Red'
Persicaria affinis............(3) + (5)

e Daylily *Hemerocallis*.................(9)

f Stonecrop *Sedum* ....(11)

g Coralbells 'Brandon Pink'
Heuchera sanguinea........(3) + (3)

h Hosta *Hosta*...............................(3)

Cutting Corner Lots—Stage Two

This stage of the design is about adding privacy to the patio area beneath the pergola and anchoring it to the surrounding landscape.

In Stage One, a Henry Kelsey rose was planted to grow on the pergola's trellis next to the garage. A bed will be placed along the patio's longest edge and a second trellis (mounted between two of the pergola's supporting posts) will support another of these roses, flanked on either side by hardy clematis. The white flowers of the 'Prairie Traveller's Joy' clematis will accentuate the red roses and will grow tall enough to spread across the pergola's cross beams. I've also selected three 'Lambert Closse' roses: a variety from the Explorer series that displays lustrous foliage and clusters of pink flowers that will also look beautiful by the patio. To keep things simple and to provide some unity, I've included another cutleaf stephanandra, Pumila spruce and more lamb's ears.

At this stage, the patio will be a pleasant place to sit in relative seclusion, and the view from the living room window will be much improved.

Front elevation view

Side elevation view

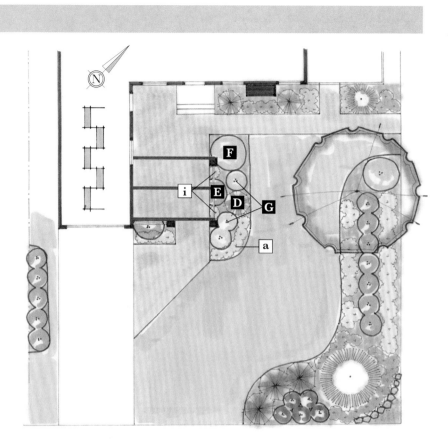

Shrubs

  D Spruce 'Pumila' *Picea abies* ....(1)

  E Rose 'Henry Kelsey'
     Rosa ....(1)

  F Cutleaf Stephanandra
     Stephanandra incisa 'Crispa' ....(1)

  G Rose 'Lambert Closse'
     Rosa ....(3)

Perennials

  a Lamb's Ears 'Silver Carpet'
     Stachys byzantina ....(5)

  i Clematis 'Prairie Traveller's Joy'
     C. virginiana x
     C. ligusticifolia ....(2)

Cutting Corner Lots—Stage Three

In this final stage of the design, the patio bed and the L-shaped corner bed will be linked to form a continuous planting. This link will further reduce the amount of lawn, soften the path to the backyard and add to the view from inside the house.

I've chosen a narrow, upright 'Columnar Scotch' pine to be positioned directly across the path from the home's fireplace. The pine's blue-green hue will look attractive against the red brick of the chimney, and a curving line of 'Gold Flame' spirea will inject a punch of colour close to the house. The irises to be planted behind the spirea won't be in bloom for very long, but will look spectacular when they are, and their foliage will create interest for the entire season. Heartleaf bergenia and two groups of blue fescue complete the bed.

The competed landscape now shows off the house to its best advantage from both approaches, and the lawn has been reduced by about one-half. Should the owners care to continue expanding the bed, they could reduce the lawn even more.

Front elevation view

Side elevation view

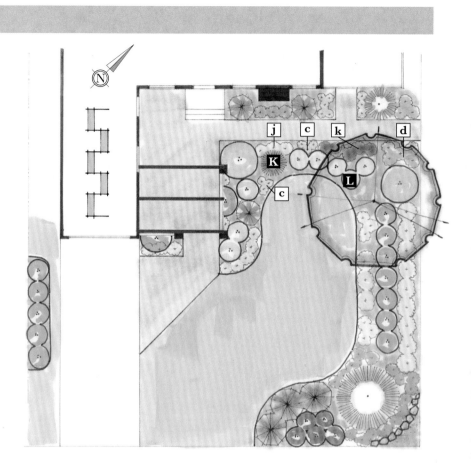

Trees

K Pine 'Columnar Scotch'
Pinus sylvestris 'Fastigiata' .....(1)

Shrubs

L Spirea 'Gold Flame'
Spiraea japonica ....(5)

Perennials

c Blue Fescue
Festuca glauca ....(3) + (3)

d Himalayan Fleece Flower
'Darjeeling Red'
Persicaria affinis ....(5)

j Heartleaf Bergenia
Bergenia cordifolia ....(3)

k Bearded Iris
Iris germanica ....(5)

Large Garage, Little Yard

Narrow front garden, prominent garage,
architecturally controlled neighbourhood,
western exposure

Wish List: de-emphasize the garage
and fulfill the architectural requirements.

*The homeowners are a young family who will likely live in
this home for many years. They've decided to spend more of
their landscaping budget on the back garden since it will be a
play space for their children and can be viewed from both the
dining area and the family room. However, before they can
turn their attention to the backyard, they must address the
landscape requirements for their subdivision, which call for
either a 40-mm caliper deciduous tree or a 2-m tall coniferous tree to be planted in the front garden.*

The Plan

Assessing the Design Options

The only part of the house proper, so to speak, that is visible from the street is the foyer entrance. Its saving grace is a relatively large front stoop and a few large windows over the visually prominent garage. Other than the view from these upper-level windows, there is no spot in the house from which to see the front garden. Therefore, the plantings will be mainly for street appeal.

The lot is narrow, relative to the footprint of the residence, so I was concerned that planting traditional shade trees would, in time, hide the front of the house from the street and make the garage even more prominent. The homeowners and I agreed that a row of tall, narrow trees along the driveway would draw attention up and away from the dominant garage and concrete pad. We also agreed that the other side of the house would require another strong vertical feature if the landscape was to appear balanced. The plan I proposed also addressed creating a view from the upstairs windows.

Landscape Tip

If you've ever wondered how four plants, each in 21cm pots, can range in price from $30 to $300, here is the answer: the cost reflects the effort and time it takes to propagate each plant. A $30 plant is probably a common plant, which is easy to propagate and grow to a saleable size in a short period of time. A plant priced at $90 is usually more difficult to propagate or takes longer to reach a saleable size. The price goes up as the propagation difficulty and growth time increase.

Stage Two elevation

Large Garage, Little Yard—Stage One

Since the homeowners are saving the bulk of their landscaping budget for the backyard, I carefully chose where money would be best spent in the front yard.

Starting with the bed along the south edge of the driveway, I have suggested a row of 'Swedish Columnar' aspen. They fit the bill perfectly and will grow tall enough to de-emphasize the garage yet stay narrow enough not to encroach on the driveway or the neighbour's property. They are also very fast growing once their roots are established, which means the couple can purchase a size that fits their budget. There is a decided depression along the property line sloping down to the street that carries away water runoff, but both the Swedish Columnar aspens and a groundcover planting of heartleaf bergenias will enjoy the moist conditions.

The next order of business will be to create appeal near the home's entrance. A gently curved bed butts up against the sidewalk leading to the backyard and borders the yard's north boundary. I've suggested a 'Weeping White' spruce be planted kitty-corner from the edge of the house. The tree's unusual narrow form will provide a strong focal point in the yard, and its mature height will balance that side of the house. Using a distinctive and formal Weeping White spruce in this first stage, sets this house apart from the others on the block; however, finding a specimen that meets the requirement set by the developer will be difficult. If neccessary, an acceptably sized Swedish Columnar aspen can be substituted.

In the rest of the entrance bed, I have plotted a curving row of low-maintenance 'Coronation Triumph' potentillas. 'Silver Mound' sage will provide a textural contrast to that of a 'Slowmound' mugo pine at the bed's westernmost end. The addition of daylilies and a repeat planting of sage will provide a nice accent.

A tiny planting nook sandwiched between the sidewalk and the side of the front stoop will be a good place for feather reed grass and some blue flax—neither of which will overwhelm the narrow space.

A budget-wise, attractive landscape will be achieved at this stage and the architectural requirements will be met.

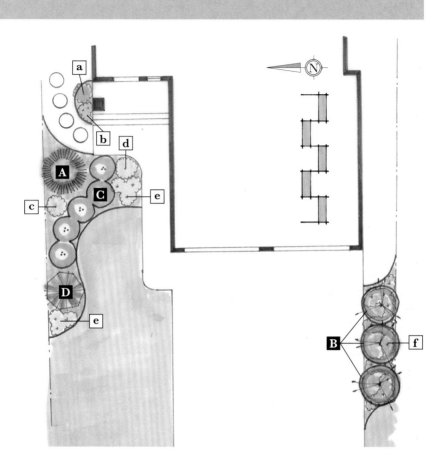

Trees

A Spruce 'Weeping White'
Picea glauca 'Pendula'...............(1)

B Aspen 'Swedish Columnar'
Populus tremula 'Erecta' ....(3)

Shrubs

C Potentilla 'Coronation Triumph'
Potentilla fruticosa..................(5)

D Pine 'Slowmound'
Pinus mugo...............................(1)

Perennials

a Feather Reed Grass 'Karl Foerster'
Calamagrostis x *acutiflora*........(1)

b Perennial Blue Flax
Linum perenne..........................(3)

c Culver's Root *Veronicastrum virginicum*
v. *incarnatum*.............................(1)

d Daylily *Hemerocallis*.................(1)

e Silver Mound 'Nana'
Artemisia schmidtiana... (3) + (3)

f Heartleaf Bergenia
Bergenia cordifolia..................(10)

Large Garage, Little Yard—Stage Two

This second stage of the design creates a bit more landscaping that the homeowners will be able to appreciate from the interior of the upper level and as they approach their property. The entrance bed will be extended to run right down the remainder of the north boundary and along the public sidewalk, coming to an end at the start of the driveway.

An ornamental, weeping crabapple is a good choice for this yard in that, when planted the proper distance from the house, its lines will be low enough not to hide the entry from the street. Its form will also provide an interesting contrast to the verticality of the other trees. The purple-pink summer flowers of a 'Dart's Red' spirea will repeat the tones of the spring blossoms on the crabapple. The addition of a 'Youngstown' juniper and the 'Pumila' spruce will provide an appealing green backdrop to the perennials, and 'Stella D'Oro' daylilies will repeat the look of the daylilies planted by the entrance. A peony will provide blooms after the crabapple. As a final touch, a boulder (with the house number on it, if desired) can be set into the planting bed and fronted with low-growing mother of thyme (see page 23 for tips on placing boulders).

Upon completion of both stages, this yard becomes appealing from all angles, will yield perennial divisions to help out with the backyard budget and will draw even more attention away from the garage.

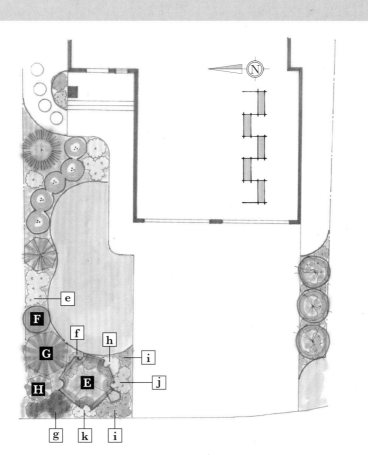

Trees

E Ornamental Crabapple 'Rosy Glow'
   Malus ....(1)

Shrubs

F Spirea 'Dart's Red'
   Spiraea japonica ....(1)

G Juniper 'Youngstown' (Andorra)
   Juniperus horizontalis
   'Andorra' ....(1)

H Spruce 'Pumila'
   Picea abies ....(1)

Perennials

e Silver Mound
   Artemisia schmidtiana
   'Nana' .... (2)

f Heartleaf Bergenia
   Bergenia cordifolia .... (3)

g Blood Red Cranesbill
   Geranium sanguineum .... (5)

h Peony *Paeonia* ....(1)

i Mother of Thyme
   Thymus .... (9) + (3)

j Blue Sage 'May Night'
   Salvia x *sylvestris* .... (3)

k Daylily 'Stella D'Oro'
   Hemerocallis .... (3)

Slopes And Other Uphill Battles

Steep slope to street, overgrown
and badly placed shrubs,
western exposure

Wish List: plants that will grow on a slope,
easy-to-mow lawn and a larger-looking yard.

*When the homeowners replaced their cracked driveway and
the path to the front of their house, their contractor suggested
they put in some stairs from the public path leading to the
front door—a wise man. Not only will the stairs provide a
more direct route to the front entrance, in the winter, they
will be safer than the sloped driveway. Having invested in
fixing the hardscaping, the owners now want to renovate the
landscape but are afraid of repeating past mistakes.*

Landscape Tip

When is a retaining wall needed? Build
one if the slope makes your property
unusable. I would consider installing one
to create a play space or an entertain-
ment area—something that could justify
the expense. Proper construction is also
essential. Without a base that's properly
compacted and leveled, the wall may
sink or heave.

Completed elevation

The Plan

Assessing the Design Options

Because this house is on a hill with a fairly steep gradient from lot to neighbouring lot, the homeowners really needed a proper plan. Sometimes I recommend retaining walls when dealing with a sloped garden. However, they are expensive, and the space here doesn't warrant one for two reasons: the front yard is not used for any activity, and a retaining wall might look out of place relative to the scale of the house. Instead, a more cost-effective and logical design option is to work with the existing grade and to use plants that have aggressive root systems or that will spread rapidly and stabilize the slope.

It is not necessary to physically remove the lawn to create a new landscape. In fact, to do so would expose the area to erosion. A better option is to kill the lawn with glyphosate (a herbicide). The main advantage to this method is that the grass's roots are left in place, which helps retain the slope. By the time the lawn's root system has completely decomposed, the shrubs and perennials should be covering the area enough to provide some protection from runoff and erosion. See page 180 for lawn removal methods.

Slopes And Other Uphill Battles

The feature tree I've chosen for this location is an Amur chokecherry with rocks placed on its south side to hold the soil. Not only will the tree benefit from the well-drained location, its multi-stemmed form will fill the empty space between the house and the neighbouring yard. Amur chokecherries look nice all year, but I think their beauty is revealed during the winter when there are no leaves covering their lovely coppery bark. Planting a tree in this location will also visually enlarge the front garden by drawing one's attention away from the house.

A great shrub for this yard is the false spirea. Not only does it have an interesting ferny texture and attractive new growth that starts off red and changes to a cream-and-green variegation, it also suckers freely, which will help hold the bank. I've also chosen 'Prairie Petite' lilacs. They are dwarf versions of the common lilac and have a lovely traditional fragrance. They too will sucker to some extent. The cutleaf stephanandra is another ideal shrub for growing in this location. Its branches will root where they touch the soil, and its leaves will provide an interesting contrast when planted among junipers. The addition of a 'Royal Cloak' barberry and a red leaf rose will add some colour next to the house.

Between the driveway and the steps is the perfect place to plant an aggressive plant like ribbon grass, as it will be well contained. It will fill the area quickly and make a pleasant rustling sound when people brush by it.

All that is needed to complete the design is a planting of vigorously growing perennials that will cover the area. With that addition, the yard's issues are addressed. The slope is dealt with, and by moving the concentration of the plants away from the pathway and towards the edge of the property, the new landscape appears larger.

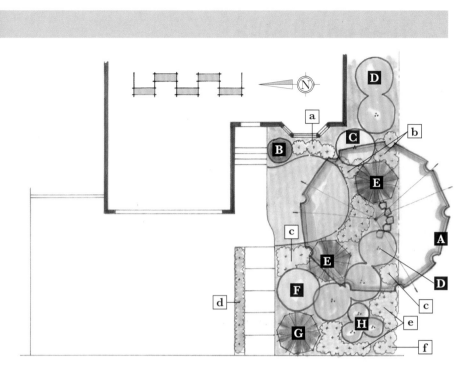

Trees

A Amur Chokecherry
   Prunus maackii ....(1)

Shrubs

B Barberry 'Royal Cloak'
   Berberis thunbergii
   var. *atropurpurea* ....(1)

C Red Leaf Rose
   Rosa glauca...............................(1)

D False Spirea 'Sem'
   Sorbaria sorbifolia ....(2) + (3)

E Juniper 'Hughes'
   Juniperus horizontalis......(1) + (1)

F Cutleaf Stephanandra
   Stephanandra incisa 'Crispa' ....(1)

G Juniper 'Wilton's Blue Rug'
   Juniperus horizantalis
   'Wiltonii' ....(1)

H Lilac 'Prairie Petite'
   Syringa vulgaris........................(3)

Perennials

a Feather Reed Grass 'Karl Foerster'
   Calamagrostis x *acutiflora*.......(3)

b Himalayan Fleece Flower 'Darjeeling Red'
   Persicaria affinis.. (3) + (5) + (7)

c Daylily *Hemerocallis*.........(3) + (1)

d Ribbon Grass
   Phalaris arundinacea ....(5)

e Stonecrop *Sedum*............:...(7) + (7)

f Blue Oat Grass
   Helictotrichon sempervirens....(3)

Putting Down Roots

Poor access, courtyard driveway, eastern exposure

Wish List: defined paths,
an attractively disguised rain barrel
and a bit of uniqueness.

*Ten year's have passed since this couple purchased their
'temporary' home, and they have now decided to stay put.
With this new sense of permanency comes a desire to fix up
their yard, which currently consists of a few tired-looking
shrubs by the front window and a sprawling Mayday tree
that is infested with black knot. While the homeowners love
the fragrance that the Mayday provides in the spring, they
have decided it has to go. They need to play catch-up with the
rest of the neighbourhood and want to start landscaping as
soon a possible.*

Stage Two elevation

The Plan

Assessing the Design Options

The main problems the design needs to address are that the front door and stoop are virtually invisible from the street, and they aren't easy to get to. The only clear view of the front door is from the driveway, and the pathway from the driveway is only 80cm wide. An enlarged landing area along the driveway will provide a comfortable space to enter and exit a vehicle but will do nothing to clearly indicate how to get to the front door from the street. Therefore, a second path will need to be constructed. All this has to be achieved in a fairly tight space, so using straight lines and 45 degree angles will make efficient use of the available area.

One way the owners can achieve the look of an established landscape more quickly is to use hardscaping elements to mimic the vertical dimension that established trees normally provide. The owners and I decided on two separate trellis features that give height but that also double as screens—one to hide the rain barrel, the other to create a courtyard feel by the front entrance.

Landscape Tip

Because a free-standing trellis/arbour needs to withstand the wind and support the weight of the plants growing on them, it's best to install it the same way you would a fence. This means anchoring the posts in concrete. Because this is a building project, you will need to locate the utilities before doing any excavation, know where your property line is and check with your local planning department for height restrictions.

Putting Down Roots—Stage One

Construction is key to this stage of the design and will begin with a deck that will project 2m from the house and have a 2.4m-wide stairway. The size of the deck allows for much better access to the entrance and for the addition of a low bench and some potted plants. The width of the stairway allows for ease of access from both the driveway and a new walkway to the street.

A partial fence with an arbour over the new walkway will accomplish the important job of indicating where the entrance is, and a 2m-wide by 3m-high freestanding trellis will be constructed 1.2m away from the house to hide the rain barrel. The design elements of the trellis, the arbour/fence and the deck railing should all match. The last stage of construction involves installing the new 1.5m-wide pathway/landing along the driveway and laying down the concrete patio slabs for the rain barrel.

A 'Mountain Frost' pear and a 'Moonglow' juniper can also be planted at this stage, as they are out of the way of construction. The pear will have lots of white blossoms in the spring, and its glossy, dark-green leaves will look quite ornamental in the summer. During the fall, the foliage will turn a nice yellow.

At the completion of this stage, the front garden will look rather bare, but if the owners undertake Stage One in the fall and begin Stage Two the following spring, they will have achieved their dream landscape quite quickly—with a short winter rest in between.

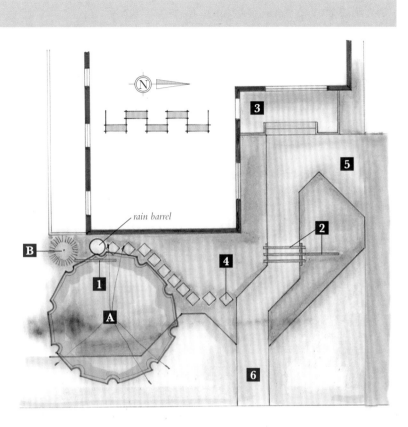

rain barrel

Trees

A Pear 'Mountain Frost'
  Pyrus ussuriensis 'Bailfrost' .....(1)

B Juniper 'Moonglow'
  Juniperus scopulorum ....(1)

Hardscape Elements

1. Trellis
2. Arbour and partial fence
3. Deck with railing
4. Concrete slab pathway
5. Landing
6. Path

Putting Down Roots—Stage Two

At this stage of the design, a 'Weeping' larch will be introduced as the garden's star. Part of it will be trained to grow over the arbour and along the partial fence. Larch are particularly attractive in spring when their needles are bright green and in fall when they turn yellow. On the opposite side of the new path, a hedge of 'Avalanche' feather reed grass, in combination with the Weeping larch, will create that bit of uniqueness the homeowners were wanting. Pairing a top graft 'Miss Kim' lilac with 'Rose Glow' barberries will give the courtyard bed between the arbour and the house lots of interest.

The angled front bed will hold 'Annabelle' hydrangea and a 'Snowball' viburnum that display similar flowers but at different times of the season. A 'Blue Lagoon' clematis will be planted on the new free-standing trellis. This variety blooms on old wood, and the vines and bearded seed heads will keep the rain barrel hidden all year and add visual interest during the winter. The other shrubs and perennials I've selected offer lots of texture and colour.

Once the garden is completed, the homeowners will have easy and direct access to the front door, a semi-private garden near the house and curb appeal that may even outshine that of their neighbour's more established landscapes.

Trees

C Larch 'Weeping'
Larix decidua 'Pendula' ....(1)

D Lilac 'Miss Kim'
Syringa patula (tree form)........(1)

Shrubs

E Rose 'Morden Centennial'
Rosa ....(1)

F Barberry 'Rose Glow'
Berberis thunbergii
var. atropurpurea ....(3)

G Spirea 'Pink Parasols'
Spiraea fritschiana
'Wilma' ....(1) + (1)

H Hydrangea 'Annabelle'
Hydrangea arborescens.....(1) + (1)

I Viburnum 'Snowball'
Viburnum opulus 'Roseum' ....(1)

J Dogwood 'Golden Variegated (Aureo)'
Cornus alba 'Gouchaltii' ....(1)

K Rose 'Therese Bugnet' Rosa ....(1)

L Juniper 'Hughes'
Juniperus horizontalis..............(3)

M Spruce 'Elegans'
Picea abies................................(1)

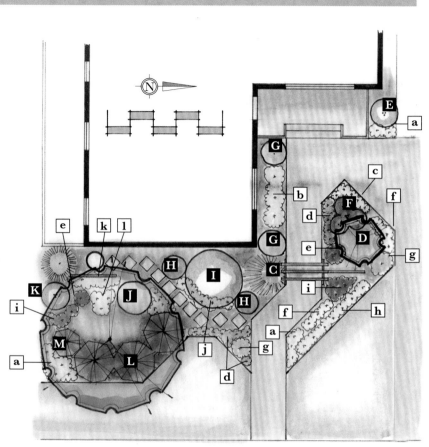

Perennials

a Heartleaf Bergenia *Bergenia cordifolia* .... (2) + (3) + (5)

b Goat's Beard 'Kneiffii' *Aruncus dioicus* .... (3)

c Greyleaf Cranesbill 'Ballerina' *Geranium cinereum* .... (5)

d Coralbells 'Brandon Pink' *Heuchera sanguinea* .... (5) + (1) + (7)

e Siberian Iris 'Caesar's Brother' *Iris sibirica* .... (1) + (1)

f Coneflower 'Magnus' *Echinacea purpurea* .... (3) + (3)

g Peony 'Highlight' *Paeonia lactiflora* .... (1) + (1)

h Feather Reed Grass 'Avalanche' *Calamagrostis x acutiflora* .... (7)

i White Beardtongue 'Husker Red' *Penstemon digitalis* .... (3) + (3)

j Garden Columbine *Aquilegia* .... (5)

k Big Petal Clematis 'Blue Lagoon' *Clematis macropetala* .... (2)

l Blue Oat Grass *Helictotrichon sempervirens* .... (3)

How To's

One of the things I've noticed working as a landscape designer is just how many people don't know the basic steps required to tackle common gardening tasks. Perhaps it's because an entire generation or two have grown up without hands-on experience or guidance from their elders—but that may also be a good thing, considering all the bad information that gets passed down from one generation to the next. At any rate, most gardening tasks are easy if you break them down into simple steps before you begin.

This "How To" section is filled with information that will walk you through all the basics—from planting a rose to caring for a tree-form shrub. My advice is to take your time and to read each how-to method before you begin to dig a hole, strip a lawn or lay out a bed. Remember, a little preparation and know-how can save time, money and even your back!

How to Plant

How to plant a rose

Before you think about digging, determine what type of rose you're planting. Is it a hardy rose or a tender one? Just check the plant tag. The type of rose you have will determine the depth to which it must be planted.

Planting hardy roses

Planting a hardy rose is just like planting any other shrub. Just be sure to dig the planting hole deep and wide enough to allow the entire root system to be buried. This sounds obvious, but sometimes the roots on a potted rose are so large that they stick above the planting medium.

Method:

1. Dig a hole three times the width of the plant's rootball and to a depth that is equal to the soil height in the pot.
2. Remove the plant from its pot and inspect the roots. If the rose is not rootbound, simply rough up the sides of the rootball to tease loose the roots. This will aid in lateral growth. If the plant is rootbound or has circling roots, slash the roots with a sharp knife and loosen them.
3. Place the plant in the hole, making sure the plant is straight and at the correct depth.
4. Backfill with loosened and lightly amended native soil. Pack the soil gently to eliminate any large air pockets.

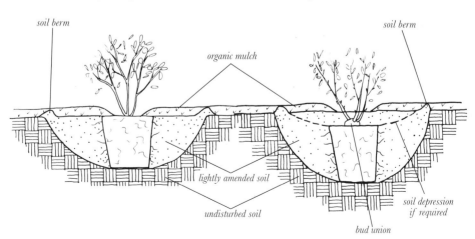

Planting hardy roses   *Planting tender roses*

soil berm

organic mulch

soil berm

lightly amended soil

undisturbed soil

bud union

soil depression if required

5. Build a small soil berm around the planting hole to retain water.

6. Water enough to ensure that the rootball and the surrounding soil are wet from top to bottom. A good guide is to use at least 5L of water for each 30cm of plant height or spread, whichever is greater.

7. Mulch with wood chips or shredded bark: 5cm deep for clay soils and 10cm deep for sandy soils. The mulch will aid in root establishment by retaining soil moisture and reducing soil compaction. Keep the stems free of mulch to avoid rot.

Bare-root roses are sold with the roots encased in wood shavings and placed in a bag. If you purchase one of these roses, be sure to plant it before the roots have a chance to dry out.

Planting tender roses
Method:

1. Find the bud union on the rose—the swollen lump at the base of the main stem where the rose is grafted to the rootstock. You need to know where it is to complete the next step.

The graft where a desired rose variety is joined to a rootstock rose is located at the bottom of the main stem and looks like a swollen lump.

2. Dig a hole three times the width of the plant's rootball and to a depth where the bud union will be 8 to 10cm below the surface of the surrounding soil.

3. Continue planting as you would a hardy rose, but if there is lots of green growth at the graft, leave a depression in the soil at that spot and then fill it in with soil when the leaves drop in the fall.

How to plant tree or shrub sold in a plastic container

By far, the most popular way that trees and shrubs are sold is in plastic pots. These pots are very sturdy and help prevent roots from becoming damaged or dried out, but they must be removed before the tree or shrub is planted. This may seem like an obvious step, but I've had customers who didn't realize the pots would not decompose or who thought that keeping the pot on would help the plant stay moist. To avoid making your own planting mistakes, read the instructions that follow.

Method:

1. Prepare the topsoil in your planting bed to a minimum depth of 30cm.

2. Dig a planting hole equal to the depth of the plant's rootball and to at least three times its width. Why not deeper? Roots need oxygen, and if the tree or shrub is planted too deeply, the roots will suffocate. Why make the hole so wide? Loosening the soil surrounding the rootball facilitates good root establishment, which is particularly important for trees. If a tree's roots can't spread, they will not be able to support the width of the crown growth and the tree may blow over.

3. Remove the plant from its pot and inspect the roots. If it is not rootbound, simply rough up the sides of the rootball to tease loose the roots. This will aid in their lateral growth. If the tree or shrub is rootbound or has circling roots, slash the roots with a sharp knife and loosen them.

4. Place the plant in the hole and ensure that the plant is at the correct depth and is straight.

5. Backfill with loosened and lightly amended native soil, and pack the soil gently to eliminate any large air pockets.

6. Build a small soil berm around the planting hole to retain water.

7. Stake any tree that is over 1.5m tall using two stakes, one on the windward side and one on the leeward side. Lightly secure the tree using proper tree strapping. The tree must be able to sway slightly in the wind to promote normal root development. Keep the tree staked for one to two years.

8. Water enough to ensure that the rootball and the surrounding soil are wet from top to bottom, using at least 5L of water for each 30cm of height or spread, whichever is greater.

9. Mulch with wood chips or shredded bark: 5cm deep for clay soils and 10cm deep for sandy soils. The mulch will aid in root establishment by retaining soil moisture and reducing soil compaction. Keep the stems and trunks free of mulch to avoid rot.

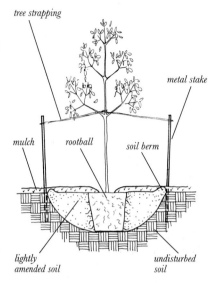

tree strapping

metal stake

mulch   rootball   soil berm

lightly amended soil

undisturbed soil

How to plant a tree or shrub sold in a fibre pot

Many trees and shrubs are sold in fibre pots, which, unlike plastic pots, decompose over time. These plants are usually field potted at the nurseries—a process that causes roots to become severed. Disturbing the few established roots within the fibre pot during the planting process may kill the plant, so be sure to follow the steps below.

Method:

1. Prepare the topsoil in your planting bed to a minimum depth of 30cm.
2. Dig the planting hole the same depth as the rootball and to at least three times its width.
3. Place the plant in the hole, pot and all, ensuring that the plant is at the correct depth and is straight.
4. Cut off the rim of the pot and any part of it that may be above the level of the surrounding soil.
5. Slash the sides of the pot. If it looks as if the rootball is falling apart, **stop** and backfill.
6. Build a small soil berm around the planting hole to retain water.
7. Stake any tree that is over 1.5m tall using two stakes, one on the windward side and one on the leeward side. Lightly secure the tree using proper tree strapping. The tree must be able to sway slightly in the wind to promote normal root development. Keep the tree staked for one to two years.
8. Water enough to ensure that the rootball and the surrounding soil are wet from top to bottom, using at least 5L of water for each 30cm of height or spread, whichever is greater.
9. Mulch with wood chips or shredded bark: 5cm deep for clay soils and 10cm deep for sandy soils. The mulch will aid in root establishment by retaining soil moisture and reducing soil compaction. Keep the stems and trunks free of mulch to avoid rot.

When the tree stakes are removed, make sure that the strapping is, too. If left, it will girdle the trunk and eventually kill the tree.

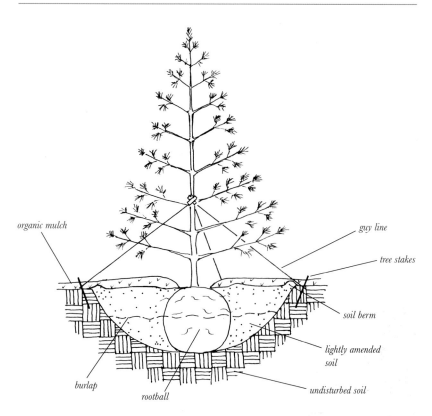

organic mulch

guy line

tree stakes

soil berm

lightly amended
soil

burlap

rootball

undisturbed soil

How to plant a 'balled or burlapped' tree or shrub

Many large trees, especially evergreens, are sold 'balled and burlapped.' This means that their roots are encased in a ball of soil that is tightly wrapped in burlap and bound with wire or strong string. Purchase these plants early in the spring before the summer heat causes their rootballs to dry out, or purchase them freshly dug in the late summer or early fall. Plant promptly after bringing them home.

Method:

1. If planting a tree, find the trunk flare—the spot on the tree's base where the roots begin to spread. You might have to remove some of the soil at the top of the rootball in order to find it. Measure from the trunk flare to the bottom of the rootball. This measurement will be the depth of the hole. The width of the hole will need to be at least three times the width of the rootball. Balled and burlapped plants are heavy and awkward to take out of a hole, so you'll want to get the calculation right the first time. Use the same calculation to determine the size of the hole for a shrub—except instead of measuring from the flare of a trunk to the

rootball, you'll measure from the crown (where the stems join at the base) to bottom of the rootball.

2. Set the plant in the hole and ensure that the plant is straight.

3. Backfill the hole one-third full. **Note:** Do not fill the entire hole! You still need to remove the wire and burlap.

4. Gently pack the soil around the base of the rootball to stabilize the tree/shrub.

5. Remove the wire or string and start to remove the burlap. If the rootball begins to fall apart, backfill the hole about two-thirds full and gently pack the soil around the rootball. You may now either cut away the burlap or open it and spread it around the sides of the hole. It will decompose. Continue to backfill.

6. Build a small soil berm around the edges of the planting hole to retain water.

7. If the tree is large enough to require staking, using three evenly spaced pegs with guy lines. Pound the pegs into undisturbed soil and use soft ties around the trunk. There should be some play to the lines to allow the tree to flex a bit in the wind to promote normal root development. Keep the tree staked for one to two years.

8. Water enough to ensure that the rootball and the surrounding soil are wet from top to bottom, using at least 5L of water for each 30cm of height or spread, whichever is greater.

9. Mulch with wood chips or shredded bark: 5cm deep for clay soils and 10cm deep for sandy soils, ensuring that the stems are free of mulch to avoid rot. The mulch will help retain soil moisture, reduce soil compaction and thus aid in root establishment.

Snip the wire or twine that holds the burlap in place and discard it. The burlap will decompose over time.

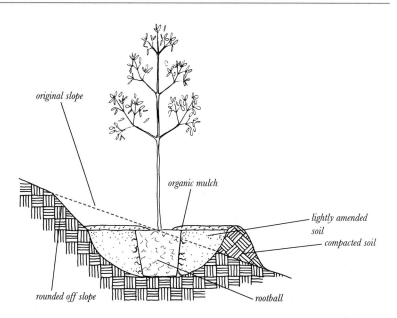

original slope

organic mulch

lightly amended soil

compacted soil

rounded off slope

rootball

How to plant a tree or shrub on a slope

Sometimes you'll find yourself faced with the difficult task of landscaping on less than level terrain. Following the steps below to create a mini-terrace on a slope will ensure soil stability and water retention in this troublesome planting area.

Method:

1. Create a level mini-terrace by cutting into the slope and using the soil removed from the cut side to fill the downward side of the slope. Compact this soil and smooth back the cut side to create a less drastic downward grade.

2. Dig a planting hole the same depth as the plant's rootball and about three times its width. Due to the contour of the space, the hole will be more oval than circular.

3. Treat the plant according to the way it is potted—follow the steps for plastic, fibre or balled-and-burlaped plants.

4. Place the plant in the hole, making sure the plant is straight and at the correct depth.

5. Backfill with loosened and lightly amended native soil. If you do not have enough native topsoil, obtain more from a landscape supplier— I don't usually recommend using bagged soil from a garden centre because it often contains too much organic matter.

6. Pack the soil gently to eliminate any large air pockets. Use any extra soil to shore up the terrace and to smooth out the slope.

7. Water enough to ensure that the rootball and the surrounding soil are wet from top to bottom, using at least 5L of water for each 30cm of height or spread, whichever is greater.

8. Mulch with wood chips or shredded bark: 5cm deep for clay soils and 10cm deep for sandy soils. The mulch will aid in root establishment by retaining soil moisture and reducing soil compaction. Keep the stems/base of branches free of mulch to avoid rot.

How to Eliminate Lawn Prior to Installing a Planting Bed

There are two basic ways to eliminate a lawn: physical removal (stripping out the lawn) and herbicidal removal (killing the lawn with herbicide). Before you can decide which method to use, you need to dig out a piece of lawn and measure how much topsoil there is beneath it before you hit clay. I strongly recommend that planting beds have a minimum 30cm depth of good topsoil.

If after digging you find you have 15cm or less of topsoil, and can't amend it without causing grade problems, physical removal of the lawn and subsoil may be your only choice. If you find you have more than 15cm of topsoil, you can opt for herbicidal removal.

Soil solarization is a lawn-removal method that involves watering the lawn area, covering it with well-anchored, clear plastic and waiting for the heat generated under the plastic to kill the grass. The method is cheap, leaves the organic matter in place and doesn't involve much work, but it can take weeks or months to work.

The method best used for removing a lawn is determined by the quality and depth of the soil beneath it and the size of the area to be removed.

Physical Removal
Method 1:

Large areas of lawn are best removed by hiring a professional with a bobcat to strip the lawn, to excavate the area to a minimum depth of 30cm and then to fill the space with good quality topsoil. This is the easiest and fastest method, and is well worth the expense, but valuable organic matter is lost in the process.

Method 2:

If the area is relatively small, lawn may be removed by hand and composted for later use in the yard. Remove the topsoil beneath the sod and retain it on site but out of the way. Excavate the clay subsoil that needs to be removed to allow for a minimum 30-cm-deep planting bed. Topsoil can then be brought in to replace the clay, and the retained topsoil can be redistributed. This method involves a fair bit of time and hard work but will save you money.

Removed lawn can be taken to municipal sites where organic yard debris is composted.

Herbicidal Removal
Method:

Sod can be killed by applying a herbicide containing glyphosate (such as Roundup). **Note:** Glyphosate does not discriminate: it kills everything. Therefore, care must be taken to prevent it from drifting onto valued plants.

Timing is important when using this method because lawn must be actively growing if the glyphosate is to be fully effective. This makes spring or fall applications less effective. Let the lawn reach a height of 15cm and then spray. This will provide a greater surface area for absorption of the product. Glyphosate leaves no damaging residual chemicals in the soil, so it is safe to plant in an area that's been treated—providing you followed the directions on the label. It takes approximately two weeks for a sprayed lawn to die back, at which point you can prepare to plant.

Because the soil beneath a lawn tends to be extremely compacted, I recommend digging a planting hole that is five times the width of your plant's rootball. Topsoil can also be added at this stage if necessary.

Herbicidal lawn removal is cheaper than physical lawn removal but involves time and labour. However, the dead grass and its root system provide a nice amount of organic matter.

How to Care for a Tree-form Shrub

Tree-form shrubs are plants pruned to a single stem or grafted onto a single stem—or both—to produce a small tree-like form. Their size makes them ideal for small yards and as features in landscapes, but they aren't cheap. You'll pay a premium price to cover the cost of creating this form, so protect your investment by caring for and maintaining it properly.

Method:

1. Remove suckers as soon as they appear.
2. Remove buds that emerge from the trunk below the desired branches as soon as they appear.
3. Until the trunk is of sufficient girth to support a larger canopy, it is best to keep the top growth compact and a bit open by thinning entire branches and pruning the tips of branches to reduce wind resistance. The best time to prune depends on the kind of plant.

I lost a lovely tree-form 'Diabolo' ninebark after a particularly windy summer. It had been in the ground for two years and I had removed the supporting stake. The crown or canopy of the plant was big and beautiful. One windy day, I noticed that the tree was bending and flexing like mad. By the end of the summer, it was dead. The inner fibres of the trunk had been ripped to shreds. Had the crown been smaller and less dense, the tree would have taken much less of a beating. Learn from my mistake.

How to Care for Borderline-hardy Plants

I like to push the hardiness envelope by trying plants that are considered borderline hardy for my area. I've been rewarded far more than I've been punished. To ensure particularly sensitive plants survive the winter, take a few extra precautions in the fall.

Method:

1. Water plants well prior to freeze-up. This may mean watering until December in some areas.
2. Mulch. A deep layer of snow is the best insulator for plants, but there is never a guarantee that it will arrive before temperatures plummet. A thick layer of winter mulch (chopped leaves, pine needles, evergreen boughs or dry peat moss) is often all that is needed to help over-winter tender herbaceous perennials. Apply mulch after the ground has frozen to avoid creating a cozy home for rodents. Remove the mulch with your hands (not a rake) in the spring when the buds on the native trees start to swell. If there is a frost warning in the spring, you may need to cover the plant with burlap or an old sheet.

English roses are considered borderline hardy in my area, so if I wanted to overwinter this lovely Gertrude Jekyll rose, I would have to provide it with protection by covering it with peat moss in the late fall.

tures, but the flowerbuds that were formed in the summer dry out if exposed to too much wind. Growing plants like these in a sheltered spot close to the house or making sure they are on the leeward side of tougher plants will help greatly. The plants on the windward side will also act as a snow fence, allowing snow to collect on the leeward side.

3. Provide wind protection for woody perennials and small shrubs. Many azaleas and rhododendrons can easily withstand our cold tempera-

4. Consider covering plants with a cardboard box weighted down with some rocks, or screen the plant with a tent made of burlap stapled to wooden stakes. In both cases, you will need to ensure that there is a gap of at least 10cm between the edge of the box or screen and the outermost edge of the plant.

How to Lay Out a Curved Bed

Many landscapes call for beds with curvy, undulating edges. These edges give a natural feel and can be designed to work around specific hardscaping features such as sidewalks. My preference is to create only a few large, bold arcs—a bunch of timid, shallow arcs are visually distracting and make lawn maintenance difficult.

Method 1:

Lay out a garden hose and move it around until you create a curve you like. Use a good quality hose—the cheaper ones get nasty kinks in them. This method works best on a hot sunny day because the heat will keep the hose pliable. Mark the curve with handfuls of flour or sand, or use spray paint.

Method 2:

Map out a curve using a homemade compass. Use a piece of bamboo for the centre with a string tied to it to measure out the radius. Pull the string taut and mark out the curve

with handfuls of flour or sand. These marks can be easily kicked away if you make a mistake. You can also use spray paint if you are confident.

The Plants

One of the most bewildering parts of creating a landscape is choosing the right plant for the right location. There are a myriad of choices available at garden centres and nurseries, but how do you best select a plant to meet your needs? Start by resisting the urge to buy a plant just because it looks beautiful. Instead, learn a bit about it by reading the label and noting key information. Also, talk to the staff. If you receive good service and they know their stuff, become a loyal customer. Developing a relationship with a good nursery that trains its staff properly will benefit you in the long run.

In reading this section, you'll note that the hardiness zone ratings are not included. Why? I don't take the hardiness ratings on plant labels at face value. These markers are, after all, only suggestions. Firstly, not all plants are tested to their lowest tolerance level for cold. In fact, I think most people would be shocked to learn just how little testing is done. Secondly, every yard has microclimates, those little pockets that offer warmth and shelter or, conversely, full exposure to the elements. I find that you can push suggested recommendations by one or even two zones in the right microclimate. The plants selected for my plans are all, in my opinion, hardy to Zone 3—some are even hardier.

Please note that the plants are listed in alphabetical order by Latin name, followed by the common name. This should help with any confusion that may result from regional naming differences. I find that Latin can be a real stumbling block for many people—hence the popularity of common names among non-professionals. If you do have difficulty locating a plant, please turn to the index on page 243.

Light in this book

Here is an explanation of what the light requirements in this book refer to.

Sun: Plants in this category need full sun all day for best performance.

Sun to P.M. sun: These plants will bloom and look fine if they receive afternoon sun, from noon until evening.

Shade: Shade plants prefer shade all day.

Shade to A.M. sun: These plants require cooler, less intense light. They can tolerate sun from morning until noon. They will also thrive under the dappled light of a tree canopy.

Trees & Shrubs

Abies balsamea 'Nana'
Dwarf Balsam Fir

A very hardy evergreen with dark-green, broad and flat needles on a dwarf form. Nice in a rock garden. Prefers a moist site. Height: 60–75cm; width: 100cm. A.M. sun.

Acer negundo
Maple 'Sensation'

Perfect for smaller yards—an extremely hardy tree with bright-green foliage that has a powdery-blue coating on the stems and buds. This tree has a slow, uniform growth habit and provides beautiful, brilliant-red fall colour. It may be bothersome if it attracts aphids; they drop honeydew on which sooty mold may grow. Avoid this problem by not planting it near patios, decks or driveways. Height: 7–10m; width: 6–7m. Sun.

Acer platanoides
Maple 'Prairie Splendor'

A Norway maple with lovely burgundy-red leaves that provide contrast in the garden. Produces showy yellow blooms in May. It turned a stunning orange the first fall in my garden and I have waited two years now for it to do it again. A very hardy tree originating in southern Alberta. Height: 10m; width: 8–10m. Sun.

Acer tataricum ssp. ginnala
Maple 'Bailey Compact'

This compact variety of maple is terrific for small yards and for screening. Foliage turns bright red in fall. It may be pruned to a bonsai-like form for additional interest in the garden. Thrives in moist soil. Height: 2–3m; width: 2–3m. Sun to P.M. sun.

Acer tataricum ssp. ginnala
Maple 'Emerald Elf'

A very pretty, slow-growing and compact dwarf form of Amur maple—excellent for small shrub beds. Deep-green foliage turns a striking scarlet-purple colour in fall. Height: 1.5–2m; width: 1.5–2m. Sun to P.M. sun.

Acer tataricum ssp. *ginnala* 'Ventura'
Maple 'Ventura'

Easily trained to many different forms with a strong tendency to be single stemmed—a beautiful feature for small yards. Produces fragrant blooms in spring and provides brilliant orange-red fall colour. If this variety is unavailable, other Amur maples that have been trained to tree form may be used. Also, shrub-form Amur maples can be trained, over time, as multi-stemmed dwarf trees. Height: 4–6m; width: 5m. Sun to P.M. sun.

Aronia melanocarpa
Chokeberry 'Autumn Magic'

A very pretty shrub with clusters of fragrant white blooms in spring, followed by purple fruit. Attracts birds and provides stunning red and orange colour in fall. Height: 1.5–2m; width: 1.5–2m. Sun.

Andromeda polifolia
Bog Rosemary 'Blue Ice'

Also known as 'Andromeda,' this plant provides nice contrast in mixed evergreen beds. Produces dusty-blue foliage on a hardy, dense, compact form and pink bell-like flowers in spring. Keep it compact by shearing and shaping when actively growing. Requires moist or wet soil. Height: 30–45cm; width: 60–90cm. Sun to P.M. sun.

Berberis thunbergii var. *atropurpurea*
Barberry 'Concorde'

Barberry is an extremely low-maintenance, heat and drought tolerant shrub. This variety is a dwarf globe-shaped form—excellent for low borders. Produces sparse ornamental red fruit and velvety deep-purple foliage with a 'bloom' like a grape. Height: 50–60cm; width: 90cm. Sun.

Berberis thunbergii var. atropurpurea
Barberry 'Rose Glow'

Extremely tolerant of heat and especially striking planted en masse or used as a contrast shrub. Yellow blooms appear in May and June and are followed by red fruit. Unique rose-pink mottled leaves mature to deep purple and turn red orange in fall. The first time I saw this shrub in its full autumn glory, I was completely sold on it. It looked like it was lit up from within. Height: 90–100cm; width: 60–90cm. Sun.

Berberis thunbergii var. atropurpurea
Barberry 'Royal Cloak'

Produces deep purple-red foliage on a mounding form—excellent shrub for contrast. Small, yellow blooms appear in June, followed by tiny, elongated, ornamental red fruit. The larger leaf on this variety makes a strong statement in the garden. Height: 1–1.2m; width: 1–1.2m. Sun.

Berberis thunbergii var. atropurpurea 'Bailone'
Barberry 'Ruby Carousel'

Dense and very thorny in habit—great as a living barrier in a formal or informal hedge. Bright-yellow blooms in May/June, followed by bright-red berries. Beautiful reddish-purple foliage with a uniform growth habit. Height: 90–100cm; width: 100cm. Sun.

Berberis thunbergii 'Monry'
Barberry 'Sunsation'

Striking planted en masse or used as a contrast or hedging shrub. Golden, glowing foliage matures to an orange cast on this compact, upright and vase-shaped plant. Produces greenish-yellow berries. Height: 90–100cm; width: 100cm. Sun.

Betula nana
Birch 'Dwarf Arctic'

A lovely native shrub with small, round, finely textured leaves. Use in borders and foundation plantings. The glossy leaves on this unusual birch make it a winner. Prefers moist soil. Height: 1–1.5m; width: 1–1.5m. Sun to P.M. sun.

Caragana arborescens
Caragana 'Sutherland'

A great feature tree for small spaces located in dry sites. This tree has a very narrow, upright growth habit and produces yellow blooms in May. Caraganas are real prairie stalwarts, and this one is particularly effective year round due to its form and interesting bark. I recommend it to clients who find other columnar trees too tall. Height: 4–5m; width: 1m. Sun.

Caragana arborescens 'Pendula'
Caragana 'Weeping'

Great heat-tolerant feature plant in shrub beds or rockeries. Produces masses of yellow blooms on graceful, weeping branches in early summer. It looks great in the winter, and is very striking when draped in fairy lights at Christmas. This grafted tree, as well as the 'Walker' variety, often has a sufficient caliper to satisfy developer's architectural requirements and is a great choice for small sunny gardens. Height: graft dependant; width: 2–3m. Sun.

Caragana frutex 'Globosa'
Caragana 'Russian Globe'

A nice tight rounded form, perfect for rock gardens and small shrub beds. Produces medium-green to light-green foliage on a slow-growing and extremely hardy plant. The brighter green emerging leaves on its new growth create an interesting two-toned effect. Heat tolerant and tolerant of high soil salts. Height: 60–90cm; width: 60–90cm. Sun.

Caragana pygmaea
Caragana 'Pygmy'

A very good choice for hot, dry locations, this naturally vase-shaped form is excellent for small formal hedges. Produces tiny yellow flowers in late spring. Its profusion of spines makes it a great barrier plant. Height: 1m; width: 1m. Sun to P.M. sun.

Clethra alnifolia
Summersweet 'Ruby Spice'

A slow-growing, low-maintenance shrub—excellent for borders or featured in small shrub beds. Prefers moist, acidic soils but adapts well to most soils and some shade. Blooms a bit later in the season than other flowering shrubs, producing 10cm, ruby-red, sweetly scented blooms in July. Height: 1m; width: 1m. Sun to P.M. sun.

Cornus alba
Dogwood 'Cream Cracker'

New growth is creamy white with yellow margins on a compact mounding form—provides striking contrast. Produces creamy-white blooms in June. This Tatarian dogwood displays deep-red new stems for winter interest. Height: 90cm; width: 90cm. Sun to P.M. sun.

Cornus alba 'Gouchaltii'
Dogwood 'Golden Variegated (Aureo)'

Bright-green foliage with creamy-yellow edges makes this a striking contrast shrub for large shrub beds. As with all dogwoods, it will benefit from regular renewal pruning to keep good branch colour. Height: best at 1–2m; width: 1–1.5m. Sun to P.M. sun.

Cornus alba 'Kesselringii'
Dogwood 'Kesselring'

Dark-green leaves on striking, dark brownish-purple stems. This variety is often pruned to a small tree form. Produces showy white fruit. Height: 2–2.5m; width: 2–2.5m. Sun to P.M. sun.

Cornus alba 'Sibirica'
Dogwood 'Siberian'

This shrub is a landscaping staple that pro-

vides interest throughout the year: dark-green leaves and attractive white fruit in summer, lovely fall colour and prominent bright-red stems in winter. Great for mass plantings and combines well with other shrubs to make an attractive mixed screen. Height: 2–3m; width: 2–3m. Sun to P.M. sun.

Cornus sericea
Dogwood 'Silver & Gold'

A very nice contrast plant that combines well with other shrubs to make an attractive mixed screen. Beautiful variegated form with bright-yellow bark that is attractive in winter. Height: 2–3m; width: 2–3m. Sun to P.M. sun.

Cotoneaster acutifolius
Cotoneaster 'Hedge'

Also known as 'Peking.' A hardy, useful shrub that is usually sheared for formal hedging but is equally as attractive left to arch in its natural form. I have seen it planted close to a garage wall and trained into a 'free-form' espalier and it looks gorgeous. Plant 30–60cm apart for hedges. Dark-green, dense foliage turns a lovely orange-red fall colour. Height: 2–3m; width: 2–3m. Sun to P.M. sun.

Cotoneaster horizontalis var. Perpusillus
Cotoneaster 'Rock/Ground'

A beautiful low-growing form of cotoneaster, often used as a dense groundcover. Its shiny, dark-green foliage contrasts with the showy-red berries it produces in the fall. Requires snow cover. Height: 20–30cm; width: 150cm. Sun to P.M. sun.

Cotoneaster racemiflorus var. soongoricus
Cotoneaster 'Soongoricus'

This is a little-known but useful and attractive shrub that is worthy of wider use. Produces blue-grey foliage and masses of white blooms, followed by showy pink fruit. Height: 1–1.5m; width: 1.5–2m. Sun.

Daphne x burkwoodii
Daphne 'Carol Mackie'

This daphne offers cream-edged, green foliage on a dense form with clusters of very fragrant, light-pink blooms in early spring. Great in shrub beds. Light sun is best; keep well watered and mulched to retain soil moisture in sunny sites. Requires snow cover for best results. Shear and shape after flowering. Height: 90cm; width: 90cm. A.M. sun.

Elaegnus angustifolia
Russian Olive

A round-headed, small tree that is also sold in shrub form. Silvery leaves and dark bark contrast well with evergreen backgrounds. Very fragrant, tiny, yellow blooms appear in June. Thrives in a hot, dry site. Height: 6–10m; width: 6–10m. Sun.

Euonymus alatus
Burning Bush 'Fire Ball'

A dwarf shrub that is nice for small sites and is easily sheared and shaped. It can be used for hedging or mass planting. Produces intense crimson-red, almost fluorescent fall colour that's so wonderful it could stop traffic. It also looks great in the winter with its ridged stems and, if conditions are right, showy red fruit. Height: 1–1.5m; width: 1m. Grows in sun or shade but develops best colour in full sun.

Hydrangea arborescens
Hydrangea 'Annabelle'

A very showy shrub. It blooms on new wood so cut it to the ground in early spring. Produces incredibly large, ball-like blooms from August to September. Moist soil is essential. Try 'White Dome' hydrangea for a slightly different look. Height: 60–90cm; width: 60–90cm. Sun to A.M. sun.

Juniperus chinensis 'Aurea' cv Gold Lace
Juniper 'Gold Lace'

Very bright-gold foliage is displayed on this semi-dwarf, wide-spreading juniper. An excellent groundcover accent plant. Height: 60cm; width: 90–120cm. Sun.

Juniperus chinensis 'Bakaurea'
Juniper 'Goldstar'

A great groundcover and contrast plant—striking when mixed with darker evergreens. Very dense, bright gold foliage—the newest growth is the brightest. Height: 30–45cm; width: 1.5–2m. Sun.

Juniperus chinensis 'Monlap'
Juniper 'Mint Julep'

Also known as 'Sea-Green,' this juniper has brilliant mint-green, fountain-like, arching branches. It is often used for trained forms like spirals. Tolerates some shade and poor soil. Height: 1–2m; width: 2–2.5m. Sun.

Juniperus communis
Juniper 'Green Carpet'

Intense bright-green new growth matures to dark green on this hardy, carpet-like form—ideal in borders and rock gardens. Height: 10–15cm; width: 75–90cm. Sun.

Juniperus communis depressa 'Amidak'
Juniper 'Blueberry Delight'

This is a dense, wide-spreading ground-cover juniper with dark needles that have silver-blue lines on their upper surfaces. Use in rock gardens—very hardy. This is one of my favourite junipers due to its variegated foliage and lovely "berries." Height: 30cm; width: 150cm. Sun.

Juniperus horizontalis
Juniper 'Hughes'

An excellent juniper for large shrub beds and is often grown as a thick groundcover. I don't recommend it for rock gardens, as it grows too wide for most. 'Hughes' displays compact silvery-blue foliage. Height: 45–50cm; width: 1–2.5m. Sun to P.M. sun.

Juniperus horizontalis
Juniper 'Lime Glow'

Feathery new foliage is lime green on a vase-shaped form. Holds its colour well and is tolerant of hot, dry sites once established. Height: 60–90cm; width: 1.5–2m. Sun to P.M. sun.

Juniperus horizontalis 'Andorra'
Juniper 'Youngstown' ('Andorra')

Very soft, green foliage that turns a beautiful plum colour in winter. A very attractive spreading groundcover juniper. Height: 45–60cm; width: 2.5–3m. Sun to P.M. sun.

Juniperus horizontalis 'Blue Prince'
Juniper 'Blue Prince'

One of the best blue-coloured groundcover junipers. Pair it with plants with gold-coloured foliage for attractive contrast in a shrub bed. Provide good snow cover to prevent tip browning. Height: 10–15cm; width: 1–1.5m. Sun.

Juniperus horizontalis 'Monber'
Juniper 'Icee Blue'

Intense blue foliage, tinged purple in fall and winter on a wide-spreading, mat-forming juniper. A great groundcover for hot, dry sites. Height: 10cm; width: 2m. Sun.

Juniperus horizantalis 'Wiltonii'
Juniper 'Wilton's Blue Rug'

A hardy and fast-growing juniper with trailing branches and silver-blue foliage tinged purple in winter. Wide spreading and tolerant of hard soil—an excellent choice for northern gardens. Height: 10–15cm; width: 2–3m. Sun.

Juniperus sabina
Juniper 'Blue Forest'

This lovely juniper sports blue foliage with branches whose ends curl straight up like a dwarf forest—makes a striking groundcover. I like this juniper so much that it features prominently in my own garden. Height: 15–30cm; width: 1.5–2m. Sun.

Juniperus sabina
Juniper 'New Blue Tam'

Striking blue-green foliage on a very dense, low, mounding juniper. Somewhat shade and drought tolerant. Height: 35–45cm; width: 3–4m. Sun to P.M. sun.

Juniperus sabina 'Monna'
Juniper 'Calgary Carpet'

This low-growing, spreading and very popular juniper has soft-green foliage and a tolerance to light shade. Once established, it prefers dry soil. Height: 20–30cm; width: 2–3m. Sun to P.M. sun.

Juniperus scopulorum
Juniper 'Blue Arrow'

This variety of juniper is extremely narrow and upright in habit, making it useful for framing entrances or as a feature plant. Displays intense deep-blue foliage on a compact form that requires little or no shearing to maintain shape. Height: 5m; width: 60–90cm. Sun.

Juniperus scopulorum
Juniper 'Montana Green'

Very dense, soft-green foliage on a narrow pyramidal form. Excellent for screening or hedging. Height: 4m; width: 1.5m. Sun to P.M. sun.

Juniperus scopulorum
Juniper 'Moonglow'

Intense bluish-grey foliage on a dense, pyramidal form that makes a great feature or screen. Considered a fast-growing evergreen that is very attractive planted in groups. Requires no shearing or pruning. Height: 6m; width: 1.5m. Sun.

Juniperus scopulorum
Juniper 'Table Top'

Intense silvery-blue foliage on a very flat-topped form. Excellent for hedging or foundation planting. Height: 1.5–2m; width: 2–3m. Sun.

Juniperus scopulorum
Juniper 'Wichita Blue'

Great for large shrubs beds, rock gardens or used as screening. This fast-growing, cone-shaped juniper displays brilliant silvery-blue foliage. Can be made more compact with annual shearing. Height: 5–6m; width: 1.5–2m. Sun.

Juniperus virginiana
Juniper 'Idyllwild'

Branches have a unique, twisting growth habit—very showy! Dark-green foliage on a strong upright form makes it a useful screening or feature plant. This juniper is a good substitute in hot areas where the look of a cedar might be desired. Height: 5–6m; width: 1.5–2m. Sun to P.M. sun.

Larix decidua 'Pendula'
Larch 'Weeping'

A very popular feature tree for moist sites, and deservedly so. Graceful, weeping branches drape over rocks and walls or crawl along the ground. Soft-green needles turn glowing yellow before being shed in the fall and grow back each spring. Height: training dependant; width: 3–4m. Sun to P.M. sun.

Lonicera xylosteum
Honeysuckle 'Emerald Mound'

One of the earliest shrubs to leaf out in spring—excellent for use in a border. Emerald-green foliage is produced on a perfectly mounding form. Produces yellow-white blooms in spring. Height: 60–90cm; width: 1–2m. Sun to P.M. sun.

Lonicera x *xylosteoides* 'Miniglobe'
Honeysuckle 'Miniglobe'

Excellent for borders and small shrub beds. Dense grey-green foliage highlights pale-yellow blooms in late May or early June, followed by dark-red, showy fruit. Height: 1m; width: 1m. Sun to P.M. sun.

Malus
Ornamental Crabapple 'Fuchsia Girl'

An excellent replacement for the very popular 'Royalty' crabapple—less susceptible to fireblight. Produces deep fire-red foliage and displays a uniform growth habit. Showy red blooms appear in May. Great spring feature in small yards. Height: 5m; width: 5m. Sun.

Malus
Ornamental Crabapple 'Rosy Glow'

A very hardy weeping form, diplaying purple-pink blooms in spring and greenish-bronze foliage. Developed from a native Alberta tree—pretty feature for small yards. Height: 2–3m; width: 2–3m. Sun.

Malus x *pumila*
Ornamental Crabapple 'Dream Weaver'

A unique columnar form that has many uses in the landscape. Perfect for highlighting entrances, driveways and sunny side yards. Deep burgundy-purple foliage highlights abundant pink blooms in spring. This tree does produce full-sized edible crabapples but due to the narrowness of the tree, cleanup is fairly easy since the fruit collects in a small area at the base of the trunk—not scattered all over the garden. Height: 3m in 5–6 years; width: 30–60cm. Sun.

Malus x pumila
Ornamental Crabapple 'Thunderchild'

A striking tree with beautiful, deep purple-red foliage and dark-pink blooms in spring—excellent for small yards. Its dark bark looks very striking during the winter. Very resistant to fireblight. Height: 6–7m; width: 5–7m. Sun.

Physocarpus opulifolius
Ninebark 'Nugget'

A choice shrub with dense, compact growth—great in small shrub beds. New foliage is golden-bronze in colour, turning later to lime green. Some of the yellow-leaved spireas, such as 'Goldmound' or 'Goldflame,' can be used as substitutes. Height: 90–100cm; width: 90–100cm. Sun to P.M. sun.

Physocarpus opulifolius 'Mindia'
Ninebark 'Coppertina'

A lovely contrast shrub with striking copper-coloured spring foliage that turns red in summer. Produces clusters of white blooms in spring followed by ornamental bright-red seed heads. Height: 2–3m; width: 2m. Sun to P.M. sun.

Physocarpus opulifolius 'Monlo'
Ninebark 'Diabolo'

A versatile plant for use in large shrub beds or as a hedge. This shrub provides nice contrast, displaying rich-purple foliage on strong, upright stems and white, clustered blooms in summer followed by interesting

red seed heads. There have been a few new introductions, such as 'Coppertina' and 'Center Glow,' which could be used as substitutes. Height: 2–3m; width: 2–3m. Sun to P.M. sun.

Physocarpus opulifolius 'Monlo' (tree form)
Ninebark 'Diabolo'

Great as a small feature tree for shrub beds—prune to maintain tree form. Provides nice contrast, displaying rich-purple foliage on strong, upright stems and white, clustered blooms in summer followed by interesting red seed heads. Height: training dependant; width: 2–3m. Sun to P.M. sun.

Physocarpus opulifolius 'Seward'
Ninebark 'Summer Wine'

A great contrast or hedging plant that displays compact purple foliage on a rounded form, which is a somewhat more compact variety than the other purple-leaved ninebarks. Produces white, globe-shaped clusters of blooms in June. Height: 1–1.5m; width: 1–1.5m. Sun to P.M. sun.

Picea abies
Spruce 'Elegans'

A Norway spruce with a dome-shaped, nest-type form—one of the first spruce to bud out in spring. Excellent for small shrub beds or borders. Use nest spruce if this one is unavailable. Height: 1m; width: 1-1.5m in 12–15 years. Sun.

Picea abies 'Nidiformis'
Nest Spruce

Great in shrub beds and borders. Usually has a slight depression on the top that makes it look like a nest. New growth contrasts with older dark-green needles on a flat-topped, bun-shaped form. This is a good substitute for 'Elegans' spruce. Height: 1m; width: 1.5m in 15–20 years. Sun to P.M. sun. I have seen them growing well under shady conditions.

Picea abies
Spruce 'Pumila'

Rich dark-green foliage on a rounded form—an excellent choice for shrub beds and rock gardens. This is a good substitute for nest spruce although it will have a different growth habit, being more globe shaped. Height: 1m; width: 1.5–2m. Sun.

Picea glauca var. densata
Spruce 'Black Hills'

This member of the white spruce family sports dark-green, very dense foliage on a conical form. A very hardy and slow-growing, ornamental, upright spruce. Defining the size of this tree (as well as many other conifers) is difficult since it will continue to grow for a long time. Height: 2m; width: 1–1.5m in 10–12 years. Sun.

Picea glauca 'Pendula'
Spruce 'Weeping White'

Soft, light grey-green foliage on a narrow, conical form with a weeping habit—a perfect feature tree for a small garden. This variety will grow to be a truly lovely specimen. I have dealt with the pest cooley spruce gall adelgid on my tree but have found that promptly removing the pinkish galls as soon as they are evident has not affected the form at all. Height: 3m; width: 1.5m in 15–20 years. Sun.

Picea mariana 'Ericoides'
Spruce 'Blue Nest'

Excellent for foundation planting or as a border plant, this spruce displays rich blue-grey foliage on a nest-like form. Pair it with shrubs with gold or variegated foliage for a nice contrast. Height: 60–75cm; width: 1–1.5m. Sun.

Pinus contorta var. latifolia
Lodgepole Pine

Alberta's provincial tree is hardy and narrow with a beautiful straight trunk. Drought and heat tolerant. Nice planted in groups and good near decks and patios, as it doesn't drop cones. One has to hope that the recent influx of the pine bark beetle will not be problematic in the future. Height: 20m; width: 4–6m. Sun.

Pinus mugo
Pine 'Mops'

An ideal, very heat-tolerant, small pine for small shrub beds. Naturally dense in habit and slow-growing—doesn't need pruning to maintain shape. 'Slowmound' mugo pine is a good substitute. Height: 1m; width: 1m in 15–18 years. Sun to P.M. sun.

Pinus mugo
Pine 'Slowmound'

Dark-green needles and upright spring candles on a very slow-growing pine. A great dwarf plant for confined sites. Does not require pruning to maintain shape. Height: 60–75cm; width: 1–1.5m in 15 years. Sun.

Pinus mugo
Pine 'Tannenbaum'

. A very hardy and drought-tolerant pine with a pyramidal form. Produces dark-green, very dense foliage from top to bottom. A beautiful dwarf 'Christmas' tree. Height: 4m; width: 2m. Sun to P.M. sun.

Pinus mugo
Pine 'White Bud'

A very heat-tolerant small pine that is ideal for small shrub beds. Naturally dense in habit and slow growing—doesn't need pruning to maintain shape. Produces attractive white candles in spring. Height: 1m; width: 1m in 15–18 years. Sun to P.M. sun.

Pinus sylvestris 'Fastigiata'
Pine 'Columnar Scotch'

Very dense foliage with a rich, steely blue colour on a very narrow form—great as a feature or for framing entrances and driveways. I have one in my garden and it spooks me quite regularly. I often think it's a person when I see it out of the corner of my eye. Height: 7–9m; width: 45–60cm. Sun.

Populus tremula 'Erecta'
Aspen 'Swedish Columnar'

Beautiful planted in groups as a screen or windbreak—good for small yards or tight spaces. This tree has shallow non-invasive roots. Small round leaves tremble at the slightest breeze on a tall, columnar, hardy form. Due to smaller lots (or is it bigger houses?), this tree is on the verge of being overused. However, its graceful form makes me think of Italian landscapes, so let it be overused. Clients often ask if this tree may be topped to keep it smaller. The answer is no. In fact, no tree should ever be topped. If you feel that this tree will be too tall for your situation, a 'Sutherland' caragana might be the tree for you. Height: 10m; width: 1.5–2m. Sun.

Potentilla fruticosa
Potentilla 'Abbotswood'

Potentillas are extremely adaptable and easy-to-grow shrubs with good heat and drought tolerance once they are established. Masses of bright-white blooms cover this variety in summer. Makes a great border plant and can be used for hedging. Height: 90cm; width: 90–100cm. Sun.

Potentilla fruticosa
Potentilla 'Coronation Triumph'

One of the largest cultivars available—great for hedging, borders or as a feature in shrub beds. Produces abundant yellow blooms in summer. Performs well in hot, dry sites once established. Height: 1m; width: 1m. Sun.

Potentilla fruticosa
Potentilla 'Goldfinger'

'Goldfinger' presents large, bright-yellow blooms that cover its dense, full form all summer. Use as a hedge or in mixed shrub beds for consistent colour. Height: 90–100cm; width: 90–100cm. Sun to P.M. sun.

Potentilla fruticosa
Potentilla 'Goldstar'

An upright bush form—very showy in beds or borders. Produces masses of large, deep-yellow blooms in summer. Height: 90cm; width: 60–75cm. Sun to P.M. sun.

Potentilla fruticosa
Potentilla 'Katherine Dykes'

A nice, dense form with somewhat grey-green foliage and hundreds of lemon-yellow blooms all summer. Makes an attractive low hedge. Height: 1m; width: 1m. Sun to P.M. sun.

Potentilla fruticosa
Potentilla 'Pink Beauty'

This potentilla presents showy, long-lasting, pink, semi-double blooms in summer on a compact, rounded form—great for borders or in mass plantings. Its flowers may fade to white during prolonged hot spells. Height: 60–75cm; width: 60–75cm. Sun to P.M. sun.

Potentilla tridentata
Potentilla 'Nuuk'

Not your typical shrub potentilla, this plant hails from Greenland and is useful in shrub beds as an attractive, spreading groundcover. White blooms appear in June and sporadically through summer. It is an evergreen shrub that turns purple in the fall. Tolerant of dry soil and lower light conditions. Height: 8–10cm; width: 30–45cm. Sun to P.M. sun.

Prunus x *cistena*
Sandcherry 'Purple Leaf'

A hardy, purple-leaved accent plant often used in mixed shrub beds and foundation plantings. Pairs well with gold and yellow foliage plants. Produces pink blooms in spring—prune annually after blooming. Prefers moist soil and a sheltered site. It may suffer from tip kill over the winter, but a good pruning of the dead branches in the spring will tidy it up nicely and by summertime you would never know it suffered any damage. Height: 1.5–2m; width: 1.5–2m. Sun.

Prunus x *nigrella*
Flowering Plum 'Muckle'

A slow-growing and extremely hardy tree that makes a great focal point for small yards. In early spring, showy rosy-pink blooms cover this tiny tree. Produces no fruit. Height: 3–4m; width: 3–3.5m. Sun.

Prunus maackii
Amur Chokecherry

A large, round-headed tree with clustered white blooms in spring and dark-green foliage that often turns bright yellow in fall. Features very attractive, often peeling, cinnamon-gold bark, which is especially eye-catching in winter months—a bonus for northern gardens. May be grown single or multi-stemmed. Height: 10m; width: 10m. Sun.

Prunus pensylvanica
Pincherry

A tree with all-year interest that can be grown in single or multiple-stemmed forms. Clustered white blooms in spring are followed by tiny, red fruit in summer. Great fall colour and the glossy, reddish-brown bark is prominent in winter. Height: 7–10m; width: 5–7m. Sun.

Prunus triloba var. *multiplex*
Double Flowering Plum

An excellent feature shrub in borders or as an informal hedge. Requires a minimum of 6 hours of direct sun to produce double, pink flowers that cover branches in early spring—prune after flowering. It may bloom only below the snow line following a particularly harsh winter. Height: 2m; width: 2m. Sun.

Prunus virginiana
Chokecherry 'Midnight Schubert'

A colourful feature tree—excellent for small yards. This small, fast-growing, oval-headed form of chokecherry has pretty, clustered white blooms in spring, followed by edible purple fruit. Green leaves turn a deep reddish-purple in early summer and have a lovely purple fall colour. This variety is not supposed to sucker. Height: 7–8m; width: 7–8m. Sun.

Pyrus ussuriensis 'Bailfrost'
Pear 'Mountain Frost'

A showy ornamental tree with an upright growth habit. Pretty white blooms in May are followed by very sparse 2cm fruit. Its lustrous dark-green leaves turn a nice yellow colour in fall. Height: 7–8m; width: 5–6m. Sun.

Quercus macrocarpa
Oak 'Burr'

Oaks should be thought of as 'heritage' trees and planted where they can be enjoyed for generations. This form has a wide, pyramidal shape, and its winter outline creates a strong presence in the landscape. I find its fall colour to be unreliable but, nonetheless, it is a lovely tree. Slow-growing and hardy, well suited to large yards. Height: 20–25m; width: 9–10m. Sun.

Rhododendron
Rhododendron 'Pohjola's Daughter'

A hardy, compact form of rhodo for small shrub beds that is an introduction from the University of Helsinki. Produces bright-white, funnel-shaped blooms in spring. Ensure that it gets wind protection over the winter to avoid desiccation of its flowerbuds. Requires moist, acidic soil. Height: 90cm; width: 1m. Sun to P.M. sun.

Salix purpurea 'Nana'
Willow 'Dwarf Arctic Blue Leaf'

A compact form of willow with purplish turning to light-grey bark and deep-blue foliage—great for contrast in shrub beds. Try it as an informal hedge. Sometimes pruned to a perfectly round ball but quite attractive left to its natural form. Prefers moist soil. Height: 1–1.5m; width: 1–1.5m. Sun.

Sambucus nigra 'Gerda'
Elder 'Black Beauty'

An excellent plant for contrast, and it holds its dark-purple foliage colour well. Produces clusters of pink, sweet lemon-scented blooms in June, followed by black berries. Vigorous growth is easily sheared and shaped. Height: 2–3m; width: 2–3m. Sun to P.M. sun.

Sorbaria sorbifolia 'Sem'
Sem False Spirea

A hardy, compact shrub that suckers easily—great for bank stabilizing and well suited to mass planting and borders. White, showy blooms appear in late June or early July. Its attractiveness is enhanced with the removal of spent flowers. An interesting substitution would be sweetfern (*Comptonia peregrina*), with its ferny texture and fragrant foliage but no showy flowers. Height: 1m; width: 1+m. Sun to P.M. sun.

Sorbus decora
Mountain Ash 'Showy'

Sometimes sold as 'Grootendorst,' this dense, round-headed tree has foliage that contrasts well with its clustered, white spring blooms and red fruit. The fruit adds winter interest, at least until the flocks of waxwings that inhabit my area gobble it up. A very hardy and fireblight-resistant variety that is great for small yards. Requires well-drained soil. Height: 6–7m; width: 4–5m. Sun.

Spiraea x *bumalda*
Spirea 'Dart's Red'

A pretty spirea with dense, rich bluish-green foliage that turns a lovely reddish-purple colour in fall. Deep purple-pink blooms appear in June and July. Many of the *Spiraea* x *bumalda* can be substituted for each other since most gardeners will notice little difference other than bloom colour. If 'Dart's Red' is unavailable, 'Anthony Waterer' or a 'Froebel's' spirea will do the job nicely. Height: 90–100cm; width: 90–100cm. Sun to P.M. sun.

Spiraea x *bulmada*
Spirea 'Gold Flame'

A great accent or contrast plant for shrub beds. Bright foliage is a blend of orange and yellow and is best in full sun. Produces light-pink blooms. Height: 90–100cm; width: 100cm. Sun to P.M. sun.

Spiraea betulifolia
Spirea 'Tor'

This shrub may not look like much at the nursery, but it makes a lovely informal hedge or border plant with clustered, creamy-white blooms in June and striking fall colours of gold, orange and bronze. It can be encouraged to bloom a second time if spent blooms are removed. Height: 60–75cm; width: 60–75cm. Sun to P.M. sun.

Spiraea fritschiana 'Wilma'
Spirea 'Pink Parasols'

A mounding plant with bluish-green foliage that is tinged red in summer turning orange-red in fall. Its foliage is more oval than other spireas, which gives it a different look. Large, light-pink blooms appear in summer. Height: 60–90cm; width: 90cm. Sun.

Spiraea japonica
Spirea 'Flaming Elf'

A mounding form—great for rockeries, perennial beds and borders. Displays tiny, yellow, orange and red foliage and produces pink blooms in June. Height: 20–30cm; width: 60–90cm. Sun.

Spiraea japonica
Spirea 'Flaming Mound'

New foliage is flaming-red maturing to gold on a compact mounding form. Dark-pink to red clusters of blooms in summer. Height: 60–70cm; width: 60–70cm. Sun.

Spiraea japonica
Spirea 'Goldmound'

A mound of iridescent yellow-gold foliage that makes a colourful accent and border plant. Pinkish blooms appear in summer. Height: 90–100cm; width: 90–100cm. Sun to P.M. sun.

Spiraea japonica
Spirea 'Magic Carpet'

A great, low-growing contrast plant that produces red, yellow and pink blooms in June and July. Shearing plants after blooming encourages branching and fresh new colour. Height: 25–30cm; width: 60–90cm. Sun.

Spiraea japonica
Spirea 'Neon Flash'

Bright-purple growth matures to dark green and turns a deep-burgundy colour in the fall. Masses of bright-red blooms borne in clusters completely cover this plant in the summer. Shearing plants after blooming encourages growth and reblooming. Height: 90–100cm; width: 90–100cm. Sun.

Spiraea trilobata
Spirea 'Fairy Queen'

Excellent as a border plant or planted in mass—great for rockeries and perennial beds. Produces abundant, white blooms in spring. I have some on the east side of my house and they flower quite well with only morning sun. Height: 60–90cm; width: 90cm. Sun to A.M. sun.

Stephanandra incisa 'Crispa'
Cutleaf Stephanandra

A finely textured, compact groundcover with reddish-bronze new foliage that turns reddish-orange again in the fall. Lovely spilling over rocks, and it roots where branches touch the soil—great on slopes. This shrub may get leaf scorch during prolonged hot spells if not kept consistently moist. Height: 30–60cm; width: 1–2m. Sun to P.M. sun.

Symphoricarpos x *doorenbosii*
Snowberry 'Marleen'

A very hardy shrub with a pendulous branching habit. Produces attractive bluish-toned leaves and pale-pink blooms June to September, followed by purplish fruits that persist into November; use in floral arrangements. Height: 1m; width: 1m. Sun or shade.

Syringa meyeri 'Palibin'
Lilac 'Dwarf Korean'

This small, compact lilac does not sucker and makes a nice feature or a lovely hedge. Its foliage has a fine texture and looks good even after the flowers are finished. Red-purple buds open to pink-purple, fragrant blooms in late spring. Height: 1–2m; width: 1.5–2m. Sun to P.M. sun.

Syringa meyeri 'Palibin' (tree form)
Lilac 'Dwarf Korean'

A dwarf form of lilac grafted to a tree form. Stunning in spring when red-purple buds open to pink-purple, fragrant blooms. Prune to maintain tree form—doesn't sucker. This form can be quite useful in a very small yard that just can't accommodate even some of the smaller trees. Height: graft dependant; width: 1.5–2m. Sun to P.M. sun.

Syringa patula
Lilac 'Miss Kim'

A non-suckering, dwarf variety whose foliage turns purple in fall—unusual in lilacs. Icy lilac-purple, very fragrant blooms open in early summer. Height: 90–150cm; width: 90–150cm. Sun to P.M. sun.

Syringa patula (tree form)
Lilac 'Miss Kim'

A dwarf form of lilac that is grafted to a tree form. The foliage turns purple in fall—unusual in lilacs. Icy lilac-purple, very fragrant blooms open in early summer. Height: graft dependant; width: 90–150cm. Sun to P.M. sun.

Syringa vulgaris
Lilac 'Charles Joly'

Good for informal hedges and screens—has a spreading habit. Produces masses of double, purple-red, fragrant blooms in spring. Even though common lilac, like this one, does sucker, I prefer it to the Preston hybrids because I love its true lilac fragrance. Height: 3m; width: 3m. Sun to P.M. sun.

Syringa vulgaris
Lilac 'Prairie Petite'

An upright, dwarf form that is perfect for small shrub beds or for use as a border plant. Produces 8–10cm, light-pink blooms in late May. Since this is a variety of the common lilac, the blooms have a nice old-fashioned fragrance. Heat and drought tolerant—spreads slightly. Height: 90cm; width: 90cm. Sun to P.M. sun.

Taxus x *media* 'Hicksii'
Yew 'Hicks'

Narrow when young, this yew's width increases with age. Its columnar growth habit makes 'Hicks' great as a feature plant or planted as a hedge. Slow growing. Requires moist, well-drained soil. Height: 3m; width: 1.5m in 10–12 years. Sun or shade.

Taxus x *media* 'Tauntonii'
Yew 'Taunton's Spreading'

This evergreen is globe shaped with a flat top. It spreads with age to form a lovely, windburn-resistant groundcover. Slow growing—requires little pruning. Requires moist well-drained soil. Height: 90–150cm; width: 1.5–2m. Shade to A.M. sun.

Thuja occidentalis
Cedar 'Brandon'

Medium-green to dark-green, dense foliage provides coverage for birds. Use as a feature, singly or grouped. Makes a tall screen. Best in a moist, humid site. If you feel that this tree will be a bit too tall for your situation, try a 'Skybound' cedar. Height: 9–10m; width: 2–3m. Sun to P.M. sun.

Thuja occidentalis
Cedar 'Holmstrup'

Windburn-resistant foliage on a slow-growing, pyramid shape—very beautiful when planted in small groups. Great for hedges, rock gardens or shrub beds. Height: 1.5m; width: 30–90cm in 10 years. Sun to P.M. sun.

Thuja occidentalis
Cedar 'Little Giant'

This somewhat columnar cedar is a nice addition to a shady border, rock garden or used as a formal hedge. It features lovely, dense, medium-green foliage. Height: 100cm; width: 45–60cm. A.M. sun.

Thuja occidentalis
Cedar 'Techny' (Mission)

This hardy, slow-growing cedar makes a very attractive, dense living fence that is wind tolerant. Its dark-green foliage, which looks coarse when young, is very tolerant of shearing and shaping. Height: 3–5m; width: 2m. Sun to P.M. sun.

Tilia americana 'Duros'
Linden 'True North'

A great tree for a small yard—a very upright, pyramidal form. Produces sweetly fragrant blooms in early summer and displays attractive white bark when young. Substitutes to consider include 'Greenspire' or 'Boulevard' little leaf lindens (*Tilia cordata* varieties). Height: 15m; width: 5m. Sun.

Tilia mongolica
Linden 'Harvest Gold'

A really nice tidy tree, this narrow, upright variety is perfect for small yards. Beautiful bark starts to peel attractively when the trunk is 5cm in diameter. Fragrant white blooms appear in summer and its foliage is green gold. If 'Harvest Gold' is unavailable, many of the little leaf lindens are good substitutes; 'Morden' or 'Golden Cascade,' with their somewhat weeping forms, are great choices. Height: 10–15m; width: 6–7m. Sun.

Viburnum dentatum 'Christom'
Arrowwood 'Blue Muffin'

A very showy shrub used as a low, informal hedge or border. Masses of clustered white blooms in late May/early June are followed by royal-blue fruit that attracts birds. I love this shrub's glossy foliage. Height: 1–1.5m; width: 1–1.5m. Sun.

Viburnum lantana
Wayfaring Tree 'Emerald Triumph'

This versatile shrub makes a superb screen, mixing well in shrub borders. Pretty white blooms appear in spring, followed by pink fruit that matures to purple-black. Leathery leaves turn rich-red in fall. Height: 1.5m; width: 1.5m. Sun to P.M. sun. I have seen wayfaring trees growing very well under fairly shady conditions.

Viburnum lantana
Wayfaring Tree 'Mohican'

This shrub produces lustrous, compact, dark-green foliage and creamy-white blooms in June, followed by edible, blue-black fruits. Fruits are excellent for jams and jellies and attract birds. Often available trained to tree form, which is quite useful in a small shady garden, but its berries need to be taken into consideration when placing it—they can make a mess on a deck, patio or pathway if the birds don't eat them off the trees. Prune after flowering. Height: 4–5m; width: 2–3m. Sun or shade.

Viburnum opulus 'Roseum'
Viburnum 'Snowball'

This compact form is great for screening. Deep-green, leathery-textured leaves turn purple red in fall, and the creamy-white blooms that appear in May are very pretty. Height: 2–3m; width: 2–3m. Sun to P.M. sun. I have seen wayfaring trees growing very well under fairly shady conditions.

Viburnum lentago
Nannyberry

A lovely shrub prized for its beautiful globe-shaped clusters of blooms that appear in May. Excellent as a feature or screen or in mass plantings—very attractive. Does not produce fruit. Height: 3m; width: 3m. Sun to P.M. sun.

Viburnum trilobum
Cranberry 'Bailey Compact'

A lovely shrub for screening or for use as an informal hedge. Dense foliage turns bright red in fall—very showy. The 'Alfredo' cranberry is very similar to this one and makes an excellent substitution. Height: 1.5–2m; width: 1.5–2m. Sun to P.M. sun.

Viburnum trilobum
Cranberry 'Wentworth'

Great for screening and large shrub beds. Blooms heavily in spring with pretty clusters of white flowers, followed by high yields of edible and ornamental red fruits that make good juice and jellies. Foliage turns a strong red fall colour. Prefers moist soil. A good substitution for 'Wentworth' is 'Onondaga' viburnum *(Viburnum sargentii)*, if you can find one, which has a purple tinge to its foliage and flowers and yellow-to-red fall colour. Height: 3–4m; width: 3–4m. Sun to P.M. sun.

Weigela florida
Weigela 'Minuet'

Dark-green, purple-tinted leaves provide great contrast. Striking, ruby-red to pink, yellow-throated, lightly scented blooms appear in early summer. Benefits from snow cover in northern gardens. Height: 60–90cm; width: 90cm. Sun.

Roses

Rosa 'Adelaide Hoodless'
Parkland Series, Hardy Shrub

This lovely hardy rose is disease resistant, producing flowers in clusters of up to 25. Hardy to Zone 2. Produces double, red, 7cm flowers with a light fragrance from June to frost. It benefits from pruning after flowering to keep it more compact. Height: 1.5–2m; width: 1.5–2m. Sun.

Rosa 'Blanc Double De Coubert'
Hybrid Rugosa

A hardy shrub rose with strongly fragrant blooms that fade and darken with age. Hardy to Zone 1 with snow cover—great for hedges. Semi-double, white, 6–8cm flowers bloom June to September. Height: 1.5m; width: 1.5m. Sun.

Rosa 'Hansa'
Hardy Shrub, Hybrid Rugosa

One of the best all-round rugosas. This variety is very long-lived and hardy to Zone 1 with snow cover. It produces double, fuchsia-red, 8–10cm flowers with a strong clove-like fragrance in June or July and repeats all summer. Height: 1.5–2m; width: 1.5–2m. Sun.

Rosa 'Henry Kelsey'
Explorer Series, Hybrid Kordesii

This lovely rose climbs with support or spreads to a wide bush. Produces large clusters of double, red, 6–8cm flowers with a spicy fragrance from July to frost. Hardy to Zone 2. Height: 2–3m; width: 2–3m. Sun.

Rosa 'John Davis'
Explorer Series, Hybrid Kordesii

This rose can be used as a striking climber (with support) or be allowed to spread. Hardy to Zone 3. It has particularly attractive foliage and is less thorny than other climbers. Semi-double, medium-pink, 8–9cm flowers bloom profusely June through frost and have a light fragrance. Height: 1.5–2m; width: 1–2m. Sun.

Rosa 'Lambert Closse'
Explorer Series, Hardy Shrub

A pretty, smallish shrub rose with clusters of 1–3 blooms. I love its lustrous foliage, which complements its blossoms beautifully. Double, deep-pink buds open to pale-pink, 7–8cm blooms with a light rose fragrance from early summer to frost. Height: 75–90cm; width: 75–90cm. Sun.

Rosa 'Morden Centennial'
Parkland Series, Hardy Shrub

A very showy rose, which is beautiful grown singly or as an informal hedge. Lightly fragrant, double, bright-pink, 7–8cm flowers bloom repeatedly through summer. Hardy to Zone 2. Height: 1–1.5m; width: 1–1.5m. Sun.

Rosa 'Morden Sunrise'
Parkland Series, Hardy Shrub

Yellow-toned roses are always tremendously popular, and this rose is a great choice for northern gardens. Striking and unusual blooms are set off against glossy foliage. Semi-double, yellow, 8–9cm flowers with orange and pink overtones bloom June through summer with a light fragrance. Height: 60–75cm; spread: 60–75cm. Sun.

Rosa, Pavement Series
Hybrid Rugosa

'Snow Pavement' Rose

A series of tough, compact roses with a low, sprawling growth habit that makes them very attractive as either a groundcover or a feature shrub. Very salt tolerant. Single to semi-double bloom forms with a light fragrance are available in shades of pink, red, white and yellow. Height: 60–90cm; width: 90–100cm. Sun.

Rosa glauca Red Leaf
Hardy Shrub Species

A very hardy and pretty plant prized for its foliage and blooms. Striking reddish-purple foliage with a blue cast highlights clustered flowers in mid to late June. Single, mauve-pink, 3–4cm flowers have a light fruity fragrance. Its coloured branches and hips give lots of winter interest. Height: 1.5–2m; width: 1.5m. Sun.

Rosa 'Therese Bugnet'
Hardy Shrub, Hybrid Rugosa

A lovely rose that is hardy to Zone 1—blooms on old wood. Produces double, medium-pink, 8–10cm flowers that are intensely fragrant. Blooms mid June, repeating until frost. Height: 2m; width: 1.5m. Sun.

Rosa 'Winnipeg Parks'
Parkland Series, Hardy Shrub

An absolutely lovely rose with almost fluorescent colour and a low, compact form. Hardy to Zone 2. Its newly emerging leaves have a strong reddish tinge, which add to this rose's beauty. Double, medium-red, fading to dark red-pink on petal undersides, 7–9cm flowers from June to frost with a light fragrance. Height: 30–60cm; width: 30–60cm. Sun.

Perennials

Aconitum napellus 'Stainless Steel'
Monkshood 'Stainless Steel'

A strongly upright perennial prized for its metallic lilac-blue flowers in late summer. Prefers moist, fertile, cool soil and tolerates partial shade. Height: 90–100cm; width: 45–60cm. Sun to P.M. sun.

Actaea simplex (syn. *Cimicifuga*)
Brunette Bugbane

A clump-forming upright plant with deep brown-red foliage and fragrant, bottle-brush-like, white flowers on arching stems in fall. Prefers a moist, fertile, organic, cool, woodland location. Height: 1–1.5m; width: 60–90cm. Shade to A.M. sun.

Actaea simplex (syn. *Cimicifuga*)
Purple Bugbane

A clump-forming upright plant with purplish foliage and fragrant, bottlebrush-like, white flowers on arching stems in fall. Prefers a moist, fertile, organic, cool, woodland location. Height: 1–1.5m; width: 60–90cm. Shade to A.M. sun.

Alchemilla mollis
Lady's Mantle

A versatile clump-forming plant that prefers well-drained soil, is drought tolerant and grows quite well in dry shade. Divide in spring. Slightly lobed leaves look especially pretty after rain. Produces lime-green flowers in late spring to fall that make long-lasting cutflowers and dry well. Height: 45cm; width: 45cm. Sun to P.M. sun.

Aquilegia
Garden Columbine

Aquilegia 'Cardinal'

A clump-forming perennial that will tolerate some shade; perfect for a natural garden. Good flower for attracting hummingbirds—freely self-sows. Available in many flower colours. Flowers appear in spring. Prefers fertile, well-drained, moist soil. Height: 30–60cm; width: 30–60cm. Sun to P.M. sun.

Artemisia schmidtiana
Silver Mound 'Nana'

Wonderful for rock gardens, borders, edging and excellent as an accent plant. Will withstand hot, dry locations. Do not fertilize. Leave standing as a nesting material for birds to carry off, or prune back hard in spring. Silky-soft, silver-grey foliage is mound forming. Thrives in well-drained, alkaline, poor, dry soil. Height: 8–10cm; width: 30cm. Sun to P.M. sun.

Aruncus dioicus
Goat's Beard 'Kneiffii'

This clump-forming perennial has finely cut foliage and plumes of cream flowers in spring. Foliage turns a fiery red in fall. Grow in a woodland garden with other shade-loving plants. Prefers moist, fertile soil. Height: 60–90cm; width: 60–90cm. Shade to A.M. sun.

Bergenia cordifolia
Heartleaf Bergenia

Many people profess to dislike this plant, but I love it. Once the ground warms in the spring, it gives an instant shot of green to usher in the season. This versatile perennial grows in a wide range of soil and moisture conditions. Its glossy evergreen foliage tints purple in winter, and pale-pink to dark-pink flowers bloom in spring atop thick stalks. Do not cut back in fall. Clump-forming in habit. Height: 40–45cm; width: 60cm. Sun or shade.

Calamagrostis x acutiflora
Feather Reed Grass 'Avalanche'

A taller variety that holds its variegation well throughout the summer. Grow as a feature plant in a mixed border and leave stems in place for winter interest. White-centred, green foliage is displayed in clumps. Seed heads appear in late summer. Tolerates poor soils but prefers moist, organic soil. Height: 90–150cm; width: 30–45cm. Sun to P.M. sun.

Calamagrostis x acutiflora
Feather Reed Grass 'Karl Foerster'

One of the best clump-forming grasses to grow as a feature plant to add height in a mixed border. Light-pink seed heads fade to tan in late summer. Leave stems in place for winter interest. Prefers moist, organic soil. Height: 90–150cm; width: 30–45cm. Sun to P.M. sun.

Calamagrostis x acutiflora
Feather Reed Grass 'Overdam'

An elegant grass in a very erect, non-spreading clump form. Leave standing through winter as it will stay upright and provide an attractive accent. Variegated foliage with pink seed heads in late summer. Prefers moist, organic soil. Height: 75–120cm; width: 30–45cm. Sun to P.M. sun.

Campanula carpatica
Carpathian Bellflower 'Blue Clips'

A clump-forming, compact plant with bell-shaped, blue to violet flowers in summer. Deadhead to prolong blooming period. Prefers moist, fertile, well-drained soil. Height: 15–25cm; width: 30cm. Sun to P.M. sun.

Campanula carpatica f. alba
Carpathian Bellflower 'White Clips'

A clump-forming, compact plant with bell-shaped, white flowers in summer. Deadhead to prolong blooming period. Prefers moist, fertile, well-drained soil. Height: 20–25cm; width: 30cm. Sun to P.M. sun

Cerastium tomentosum
Snow-in-Summer

A great groundcover for poor soils and dry slopes. This mat-forming, spreading plant has woolly, grey foliage and pretty white flowers from late spring to early summer. Not usually recommended for use in 'manicured' rock gardens as controlling its spread can be a little difficult. Prefers dry, well-drained soil. Height: 15–20cm; width: 90–100+cm. Sun.

Clematis macropetala
Big Petal Clematis 'Blue Bird'

Produces a lush, pest-free screen—very hardy. Grow as a climber with support, as a groundcover or trailing over walls. Developed by Frank Skinner of Manitoba in 1962. Mauve-blue, semi-double flowers with cream-white centres bloom in spring. Prefers fertile, well-drained soil and cool roots. Do not cut back. Height: 2.5–3m; width: 1–2m. Sun to P.M. sun.

Clematis macropetala
Big Petal Clematis 'Blue Lagoon'

Produces a lush, pest-free screen—very hardy. Grow as a climber with support, as a groundcover or trailing over walls. Deep-blue flowers appear in spring. Prefers fertile, well-drained soil and cool roots. Do not cut back. Height: 2–3m; width: 1–2m. Sun to P.M. sun.

Clematis macropetala
Big Petal Clematis 'Rosy O'Grady'

Produces a lush, pest-free screen—very hardy. Grow as a climber with support, as a groundcover or trailing over walls. Bell-shaped, mauve-pink flowers appear in spring, followed by attractive seed heads. Prefers well-drained, fertile soil and cool roots. Do not cut back. Height: 3–5m; width: 1–2m. Sun.

Clematis virginiana x *C. ligusticifolia*
Clematis 'Prairie Traveller's Joy'

A very hardy, vigorous climber that tolerates most garden soils. Grow in a wild garden in and around trees or shrubs. Developed by Frank Skinner in Manitoba in 1962. Star-like, white flowers cover the plant in summer to fall, followed by pretty seed heads. Prefers fertile, well-drained soil. Height: 3–4m; width: 2–3m. Sun to P.M. sun.

Clematis viticella
Virgin's Bower Clematis 'Polish Spirit'

Makes a hardy, lush, pest-free and easy-to-grow screen. It needs a support and cool roots. Purple-blue flowers in summer are followed by very attractive seed heads. Cut back in late fall. Thrives in fertile, well-drained soil. Height: 2.5–3m; width: 1–2m. Sun to P.M. sun.

Coreopsis verticillata
Threadleaf Tickseed 'Zagreb'

A clump-forming, compact plant with fine foliage and golden-yellow flowers from early summer to fall. Prefers fertile, well-drained soil. Don't plant it where water may pool in spring. Deadhead for more blooms. Height: 25–40cm; width: 30cm. Sun to P.M. sun.

Corydalis flexuosa
Blue Fumitory 'China Blue'

A mounding perennial with fern-like foliage. Produces tubular purple-blue flowers late spring to summer—cut back to extend bloom. Prefers fertile, well-drained soil. Height: 20–30cm; width: 45–60cm. Shade to A.M. sun.

Dianthus deltoides
Maiden Pink

Dainty double flowers bloom in summer on an evergreen, mat-forming plant—do not cut back. Self-sows freely. Prefers moist, well-drained, alkaline soil—avoid winter wet. Height: 15–20cm; width: 25–45cm. Sun to P.M. sun.

Dianthus plumarius
Cottage Pinks

A traditional perennial for the rock garden or perennial border. Makes a good cutflower—deadhead to prolong blooms. Fragrant, semi-double to double flowers in varied colours bloom in late spring to early summer on an evergreen, clump-forming plant—do not cut back. Prefers moist, well-drained, alkaline soil—avoid winter wet. Height: 20–40cm; width: 30–40cm. Sun to P.M. sun.

Dicentra
Pacific Bleeding Heart 'King of Hearts'

A pretty clump-forming perennial with fern-like foliage. It can be divided in spring or when the plant goes dormant. Use as a groundcover in a woodland garden. Dark-rose flowers appear in spring to summer. Avoid hot and windy sites. Prefers fertile, moist, well-drained, organic soil. Height: 15–25cm; width: 30–45cm. Shade to A.M. sun.

Dicentra formosa
Fernleaf Bleeding Heart

Use this clump-forming plant as a groundcover in a woodland garden. Produces attractive, fern-like foliage that highlights pink flowers that bloom from mid spring to late summer. Prefers moist, well-drained, fertile, organic soil—avoid hot and windy sites. Height: 30–45cm; width: 45–60cm. Shade to A.M. sun.

Dicentra spectabilis
Goldleaf Bleeding Heart 'Goldheart'

A pretty groundcover with striking lime-green foliage for use in a woodland garden. It will go dormant in sunny hot locations. Produces pink flowers in spring to early summer and prefers moist, well-drained, fertile, organic soil. Height: 75–90cm; width: 75–90cm. Shade to A.M. sun.

Dictamnus albus v. purpureus
Purple Gas Plant

One of the longest living perennials, *Dictamus* produces an abundance of fragrant pink flowers in late spring to early summer. May take a few years to bloom. The plants are late to come up in the spring; do not disturb too early. Thrives in dry, moderately fertile, well-drained soil. Clump-forming in habit. Height: 75–90cm; width: 60–75cm. Sun to P.M. sun.

Delphinium
Delphinium

Delphiniums are the pride of many northern (particularly Prairie) gardeners. They add a strong upright statement to perennial borders and are traditional favourites. Pacific Giant, Clansman and New Millennium are just a few of the excellent series of widely available delphiniums. This perennial's upright habit benefits from a wind-sheltered location and may require staking. Divide every 3 to 4 years and cut back after flowering to promote re-blooming. Delphiniums are heavy feeders and benefit from regular fertilizing. Spikes of dark-blue, white, mauve, pink and—recently introduced—red flowers appear in summer. Prefers moist, fertile, well-drained soil. Height: 1–1.5+m; width: 75–90cm. Sun to P.M. sun.

Echinacea
Coneflower 'Kim's Knee High'

A dwarf form of the purple coneflower. Displays fragrant, reflexed, pink flowers with a red-orange central disk in summer. Prefers well-drained soil. Height: 50–60cm; width: 30–45cm. Sun to P.M. sun.

Echinacea purpurea
Purple Coneflower 'Magnus'

An award-winning variety with petals that are more horizontal than other coneflowers. Flat, purple flowers with a dark-orange central disk bloom summer to fall on a clump-forming plant. Drought tolerant once established. Prefers well-drained soil. Height: 60–90cm; width: 45cm. Sun to P.M. sun.

Echinacea purpurea
Purple Coneflower

Coneflowers are wonderful clump-forming perennials for any mixed border and are another traditional favourite in northern gardens, partly because they provide colour in the late summer landscape, but also because they hold up well to heat and wind. Coneflowers attract butterflies and make excellent cutflowers. Flower petals are reflexed and have attractive prominent centres. Varieties are available in mauve, light mauve, white and coral shades but the mauve are still the hardiest. They bloom in summer to fall. Prefers well-drained soil. Height: 50–100cm; width: 30–45cm. Sun to P.M. sun.

Epimedium x rubrum
Bishop's Hat

A useful rhizomatous perennial groundcover that is clump forming. Young foliage is tinted red and provides some fall colour. Produces ruby-red flowers in spring. Prefers moist, organic, well-drained soil but tolerates poor soils and dry sites. Height: 25–40cm; width: 30–45cm. Shade to A.M. sun.

Eupatorium purpureum
Sweet Joe Pye

One of the showiest perennials! It forms a large, clump-forming, upright bush that contrasts well with evergreens and attracts butterflies. Fragrant, clustered, rose-purple flowers bloom late in summer to fall. There is also a white flowering variety 'Bartered Bride' that is quite striking. Prefers moist, alkaline soil. Height: 90–50cm; width: 90–100cm. Sun to P.M. sun.

Festuca glauca
Blue Fescue

A wonderful clump-forming accent plant to use with evergreens. You'll find them sold along with an ever-widening choice of grasses at most garden centres. Blue-green foliage produces blue-green seed heads in summer. Prefers well-drained, dry soil. Height: 25–40cm; width: 25–30cm. Sun to P.M. sun.

Festuca glauca
Blue Fescue 'Elijah Blue'

A tightly clump-forming accent plant—great to use with evergreens. Snip blades to accent cutflower arrangements. Fine-textured, powder-blue foliage produces dainty, blue-green seed heads in summer. Prefers well-drained, dry soil. Height: 15–20cm; width: 30–40cm. Sun to P.M. sun.

Gaillardia
Blanket Flower 'Baby Cole'

A colourful, clump-forming perennial. Produces red and yellow flowers with maroon centres from summer to fall that attract butterflies. Tolerant of poor soils but prefers fertile, dry, well-drained soil. Height: 15–20cm; width: 15–20cm. Shade to P.M. sun.

Geranium
Cranesbill 'Johnson's Blue'

Good for use as a groundcover to control weeds, even in dry shade. Displays a spreading habit with aromatic foliage and good fall colour. Produces lavender-blue flowers in early summer. Prefers well-drained soil. Height: 30–45cm; width: 60–75cm. Sun or shade.

Geranium
Cranesbill 'New Dimension'

A spreading perennial that is good for use as a groundcover to control weeds, even in dry shade. Foliage is aromatic and turns bronze yellow in fall. Purple-blue flowers appear in early summer. Prefers well-drained soil. Cut down after flowering to promote new growth. Height: 30cm; width; 45–60cm. Sun to P.M. sun.

Geranium cinereum
Greyleaf Cranesbill 'Ballerina'

Perennial geraniums are undemanding, long-lived plants, suitable as a groundcover for a woodland or shrub bed. Clump-forming in habit and easily divided. 'Ballerina' has red-veined, lilac-pink flowers with red centres that bloom in late spring to summer and grey-green foliage. Prefers well-drained soil. Height: 10–15cm; width: 20–30cm. Sun to P.M. sun.

Geranium sanguineum
Blood Red Cranesbill

A spreading perennial, suitable as a groundcover. Easy to divide. Remove spent blooms to encourage new growth. Prefers well-drained soil. Height: 15–20cm; width: 25–30cm. Sun to P.M. sun.

Geranium macrorrhizum
Bigroot Cranesbill

An undemanding, long-lived perennial. Produces pink to purplish-pink flowers in early summer and aromatic foliage. Has a spreading habit. Prefers well-drained soil and tolerates dry shade. Height: 30–40cm; width: 45–60cm. Sun to P.M. sun.

Helianthus
Thin Leaf Sunflower 'Capenoch Star'

A tall, upright, clump-forming plant that is valued for its late season blooms. Use at the back of borders. Produces lemon-yellow flowers from late summer to fall. Prefers fertile, organic, well-drained, moist soil. Height: 1–1.5m; width: 60–90cm. Sun to P.M. sun.

Helictotrichon sempervirens
Blue Oat Grass

Grasses offer texture, variety of form and a sense of movement in the garden. This grass provides excellent contrast with other perennials or shrubs, particularly those with purple, yellow or silver foliage. Clump-forming in habit with blue, spiky foliage and arching, tan seed heads in summer. Prefers fertile, well-drained, alkaline soil. Height: 90–100cm; width: 60cm. Sun to P.M. sun.

Heliopsis helianthoides
False Sunflower

This large, clump-forming perennial is suitable for any mixed border, and its blooms make excellent cutflowers. Single or double, golden-yellow flowers appear midsummer to fall. Prefers fertile, well-drained, moist, organic soil. Height: 1–1.5m; width: 60cm. Sun.

Heliopsis helianthoides var. *scabra*
False Sunflower 'Summer Sun'

This large, clump-forming perennial is suitable for any mixed border, and its blooms make excellent cutflowers. This variety is a little shorter and more compact. Single or semi-double, golden-yellow flowers appear midsummer to fall. Prefers fertile, well-drained, moist, organic soil. Height: 75–90cm; width: 45–60cm. Sun to P.M. sun.

Hemerocallis
Daylily

Daylilies are hardy, versatile, clump-forming plants with grass-like foliage. They are ideal for any mixed border and benefit from dividing every 3 to 5 years. Flowers appear in late spring to late summer. Some varieties bloom more than once and some have blooms that last for longer than one day. Because there are so many stunning varieties of daylilies, I hesitate to specify a particular variety since doing so may cause a gardener to restrict his or her choices. Some of my personal favourites are 'Chicago Apache, 'Flasher' 'Hyperion' and 'Stella de Oro.' I suggest that gardeners choose a daylily that they find appealing. Prefers moist, fertile, well-drained soil. Heights range: 50–95cm; width: 45–90cm Sun to P.M. sun.

Hemerocallis
Daylily 'Chicago Apache'

A lovely daylily with grass-like, clump-forming foliage. Ruffled, deep scarlet-red flowers appear mid season. Prefers moist, fertile, well-drained soil. Height: 60cm; width: 45–75cm. Sun to P.M. sun.

Hemerocallis
Daylily 'Flasher'

A lovely daylily with grass-like, clump-forming foliage. Bright-tangerine flowers appear early in the season. Prefers moist, fertile, well-drained soil. Height: 70cm; width: 45–75cm. Sun to P.M. sun.

Hemerocallis
Daylily 'Hyperion'

A classic daylily with grass-like, clump-forming foliage. An extended bloomer—fragrant flowers last longer than a single day. Lemon-yellow flowers appear in mid season. Prefers moist, fertile, well-drained soil. Height: 95cm; width: 45–90cm. Sun to P.M. sun.

Hemerocallis
Daylily 'Stella de Oro'

A short, clump-forming daylily that produces golden-yellow flowers continuously summer to fall. Its fragrant flowers last longer than a single day. This daylily is well suited to smaller beds, borders or for use in raised beds. Prefers moist, fertile, well-drained soil. Height: 30cm; width: 30–60cm. Sun to P.M. sun.

Heuchera
Coralbells

Heuchera 'Petite Pearl Fairy'

An attractive, clump-forming plant with pretty foliage and tiny blooms held atop the foliage on stalks in late spring to early summer. May require replanting every 2 years in fall, as crowns tend to push upwards. Requires moist, fertile, well-drained soil. Height: 40–60cm; width: 30–60cm. Purple-leaved varieties: Shade to A.M. sun. Green-leaved varieties: Sun to P.M. sun.

Heuchera
Coralbells (Alumroot) 'Chocolate Ruffles'

Heucheras are hardy plants that are prized for their attractive foliage and tiny blooms. Clump-forming in habit, this variety displays huge, ruffled, chocolate and burgundy foliage and tiny, white flowers on 75cm-tall stalks in summer. Prefers moist, fertile, well-drained soil. Height: 40–45cm; width: 60cm. Shade to A.M. sun.

Heuchera sanguinea
Coralbells 'Brandon Pink'

An attractive, clump-forming plant with attractive green and white foliage and tiny rose-pink blooms held atop the foliage on stalks in late spring. May require replanting every 2 years in fall, as crowns tend to push upwards. Requires moist, fertile, well-drained soil. Height: 40–60cm; width: 60cm. Sun to P.M. sun.

Heuchera
Coralbells 'Strawberry Candy'

An attractive, clump-forming plant with silver-marbled, green foliage and tiny pink blooms held atop the foliage on 40cm stalks in summer. May require replanting every 2 years in fall, as crowns tend to push upwards. Requires moist, fertile, well-drained soil. Height: 25cm; width: 45cm. Sun to P.M. sun.

Hosta
Hosta

Hostas are wonderful perennials. They are hardy, attractive and easy to grow. There are well over a thousand varieties collected by gardeners all over the world. Although I have specified varieties in the landscape designs in this book, you will find many more varieties to choose from at your local garden centre, so don't let my choices keep you from experimenting with varieties similar in size to those I have suggested.

Hosta
Hosta 'Francee'

This is an elegant, award-winning variety that makes a great groundcover. It has forest-green, heart-shaped foliage edged in white. Prefers moist, fertile, well-drained, organic, slightly acidic soil. Height: 55cm; width: 1m. Shade to A.M. sun.

Hosta
Hosta 'Patriot'

Grown for its attractive clumping form and dark-green foliage with white margins. Produces lavender blooms in summer. Prefers moist, fertile, well-drained, organic, slightly acidic soil. Height: 60cm; width: 1m. Shade to A.M. sun.

Hosta
Hosta 'Golden Tiara' ('Kugotia')

A fast growing but small hosta that can be used as a groundcover or as an edging plant. Light-green foliage has gold margins. Prefers moist, fertile, well-drained, organic, slightly acidic soil. Height: 40cm; width: 95cm. Shade to A.M. sun.

Hosta
Hosta 'Sum and Substance'

One of the largest hostas, it is quite slug resistant. Thick, lemon-green, cupped foliage produces lavender flowers in summer—needs some sun for best colour. Prefers moist, fertile, well-drained, organic, slightly acidic soil. Height: 75cm; width: 1.5+m. Shade to A.M. sun.

Hosta sieboldiana
Hosta 'Frances Williams'

One of the larger hostas. Displays thick, puckered, blue-green foliage with gold margins; performs best in shade. Considered somewhat slug resistant. Prefers moist, fertile, well-drained, organic, slightly acidic soil. Height: 70cm; width: 1.5m. Shade to A.M. sun.

Iris
Dwarf Bearded Iris

Iris 'Boo'

These tiny irises are just like their larger counterparts in looks but are better suited to the front of a border or in a rock garden. I like the variety 'Boo' among many others. Available in a variety of colours. Blooms in spring. Prefers moist, well-drained, gritty soil. Avoid winter wet. Height: 15–40cm; width: 30–45cm. Sun.

Iris germanica
Bearded Iris 'Loganberry Squeeze'

Irises provide wonderful colour in the spring with spectacular flowers, and fans of foliage add interest throughout the growing season. Clump-forming and upright in habit, they are easily divided. 'Loganberry Squeeze' (just one of hundreds of varieties) produces fragrant, raspberry-violet flowers that bloom in early summer. Prefers moist, well-drained, fertile soil. Height: 90cm; width: 45–60cm. Sun.

Iris sibirica
Siberian Iris 'Caesar's Brother'

One of the least demanding of all irises, this long-lived perennial is lovely around ponds or in Japanese gardens. 'Caesar's Brother' produces deep-purple flowers in late spring. Prefers well-drained, moist, slightly acidic soil. Avoid dry sites. Height: 75–90cm; width: 30–45cm. Sun to P.M. sun.

Liatris spicata
Liatris

An upright, clump-forming perennial that makes an excellent cutflower and attracts bees and butterflies to the garden. Produces spikes of purple flowers in late summer. Prefers moist, well-drained, moderately fertile soil. Height: 60–90cm; width: 30–45cm. 'Kobold' is a slightly shorter variety useful for the front of borders (height: 45–60cm; width: 30–45cm). Sun to P.M. sun.

Ligularia
Rayflower 'The Rocket'

Large tropical-looking leaves with black stems are displayed on this clump-forming, upright plant. Spikes of bright-yellow flowers bloom in summer. Avoid bright, windy sites. Requires very moist, deep, moderately fertile soil. Height: 1.2–1.8m; width: 75–90cm. Shade to A.M. sun.

Lilium
Asiatic Lily, Pixie Series

Lilium 'Crimson Pixie'

A wonderful addition to any perennial bed, the Pixie series offers a variety of shorter, clump-forming lilies with blooms in many colours. Most flower midsummer and are quite hardy. Prefers fertile, well-drained, organic soil and to have their base shaded. Height: 25cm; width: 30–45cm. Sun to P.M. sun.

Lilium martagon
Martagon Lily 'Gay Lights'

Martagon lilies are very striking and hardy perennials. 'Gay Lights' is a tall, elegant lily that produces abundant blooms of recurved, yellow-brown flowers with maroon spots in early summer. Requires cool, well-drained, moist, organic soil. Height: 1.2–1.5m; width: 30–45cm. Sun to P.M. sun.

Limonium platyphyllum (syn *L. latifolium*)
Sea Lavender

Wonderful billowy sprays of flowers—excellent for cutting or drying. Suitable for a mixed border. Tiny, light-violet flowers bloom midsummer to late summer. Well-drained, sandy soil. Grows best in lean soil. Height: 45–60cm; width: 45–60cm. Sun to P.M. sun.

Linum perenne
Perennial Blue Flax

A clump-forming plant covered in striking but dainty, sky-blue flowers that last one day each, produced over a long period in summer. Allow to self-seed. Prefers moist, well-drained soil. Height: 40–60cm; width: 30–45cm. Sun to P.M. sun.

Monarda
Beebalm 'Marshall's Delight'

A clump-forming plant suitable for the mixed border and attractive to bees and hummingbirds. Produces aromatic foliage and is long blooming with large, rose-pink flowers in summer. This variety is highly mildew-resistant. Does best in moist, moderately fertile, well-drained soil. Height: 60–90cm; width: 45–60cm. Sun to P.M. sun.

Paeonia
Peony

Peony 'Cincinnati'

The peony is one of the best and easiest perennials to grow. Not only does it have great ornamental value, but it is also hardy and long-lived. Peonies have a variety of flower forms ranging from single to semi-double, Japanese to fully double. The foliage is just as interesting, ranging from fern-like to deeply lobed. I prefer the single-flowering varieties since they tend to flop less than the double-flowering types, and the brightly coloured stamens on the single flowers give a showier look to my eye, but I still recommend all types. By the time I think to put peony supports on my double-flowering one, it is often too late to get them around the already huge plant. Like other perennials, there are lots to choose from, so gardeners should select a variety they find appealing. Prefers fertile, moist, well-drained, acid-free soil. Avoid using high nitrogen fertilizers; add bonemeal in spring and fall. Height: 35–95cm; width: 60–100cm. Sun to P.M. sun.

Paeonia Hybrid Group
Peony

Peony 'Coral Charm'

The hybrid group of peonies is generally more compact, bloom a bit earlier and have thick stems that hold up well to adverse weather conditions. 'Coral Charm' displays semi-double, coral-peach flowers in spring. Prefers moist, acid-free, fertile, well-drained soil. Plant eyes 5cm deep or less. Height: 90cm; width: 75cm–1m. Sun to P.M. sun.

Paeonia lactiflora
Peony 'Highlight'

A slow-growing but long-lived, clump-forming perennial. Add wire hoop early for extra support. Produces double, velvety dark-red flowers in spring. Prefers moist, acid-free, fertile, well-drained soil. Plant eyes 5cm deep or less. Height: 90cm; width: 90–100cm. Sun to P.M. sun.

Penstemon digitalis
White Beardtongue 'Husker Red'

An upright plant with dark burgundy-bronze foliage and cream-white flowers (sometimes tinted purple)—irresistible to hummingbirds. Blooms in summer and is drought tolerant but prefers fertile, well-drained soil. Height: 50–75cm; width: 20–30cm. Sun to P.M. sun.

Persicaria affinis
Himalayan Fleece Flower 'Darjeeling Red'

A long-blooming evergreen groundcover that produces spikes of pink flowers that age to burnt red and foliage that turns red in fall. Flowers from midsummer to fall. Great for front borders. Grows in a moist or dry area but prefers moist, fertile soil to produce a denser mat of foliage. Height: 15–25cm; width: 60–90+cm. Sun to P.M. sun.

Phalaris arundinacea var. *picta*
Ribbon Grass

This vigorous grass has interesting white-striped foliage and creamy seed heads that appear in summer. Contain to prevent unwanted spread. Prefers moist, well-drained soil. Height: 60–70cm; width: 60–90cm. Sun to P.M. sun.

Physostegia virginiana
Obedient Plant

Plants stand up well to wind and produce lilac to purple-pink flowers in midsummer to fall—lovely as a cutflower. Has a spreading, upright habit with dark-green, willowy foliage. Prefers moist, fertile soil. Height: 60–100cm; width: 45–60cm. Sun.

Polygonatum
Solomon's Seal

This clump-forming, upright plant has attractive arching stems with pretty white flowers in spring—excellent for woodland gardens. Prefers moist, well-drained, organic soil. Height: 45–60cm; width: 45–60cm. Shade to A.M. sun.

Primula auricula
Auricula Primrose

A very hardy primrose for northern climates. Fragrant blooms appear in spring and are available in single and double forms and in many colours. Clump forming in habit—do not cut back. Requires moist, well-drained, organic soil—avoid winter wet. Height: 15–25cm; width: 20–30cm. Shade to A.M. sun.

Pulmonaria saccharata
Bethlehem Sage 'Argentea'

Pulmonarias are very tough, clump-forming plants that are well suited as groundcovers for a woodland or border edging. Red flowers fading to blue appear in spring, but these plants are prized mostly for their heavily frosted, silver foliage. Prefers fertile, well-drained, organic soil but will tolerate poor soil. Height: 20–30cm; width: 45–60cm. Shade to A.M. sun.

Pulsatilla patens (syn *Anemone patens*)
Prairie Crocus

Native prairie crocus is clump-forming in habit with fern-like foliage and lovely blooms that become fluffy seed heads. Mauve-pink flowers, sometimes cream, appear in early spring. It resents being moved. Prefers moist, sharply drained, fertile soil. Height: 10–15cm; width: 10–20cm. Sun to P.M. sun.

Rudbeckia fulgida var. sullivantii
Black-Eyed Susan 'Goldsturm'

Produces masses of deep-yellow, daisy-like flowers with dark-brown centres all summer and into fall. Great for cutflowers. Drought tolerant and grows well in poor soil but prefers moist, well-drained and fertile soil. Height: 45–60cm; width: 30–45cm. Sun.

Salvia nemorosa
Blue Sage 'East Friesland'

Clump forming with a compact habit, this plant is suitable for a mixed border. Violet-blue flowers in summer are good as a cutflowers. Cut back after blooming for second flush of flowers. Thrives in well-drained, moist, organic soil. Height: 45–60cm; width: 45–60cm. Sun to P.M. sun.

Salvia x sylvestris
Blue Sage 'May Night'

This clump-forming, upright perennial produces very long-lasting blooms that make good cutflowers. Fragrant blue-violet flowers appear in summer. Try cutting back after initial bloom to promote re-blooming. Does best in well-drained, moist, organic soil. Height: 60–75cm; width: 45–60cm wide. Sun to P.M. sun.

Sedum
Stonecrop (Creeping Sedum)

Sedum 'Blue Spruce'

Creeping sedums grow quickly and adapt to poor soils and dry periods. They make good groundcovers and are available with a wide range of interesting-looking foliage: 'Blue Spruce' is a variety with blue, needle-like foliage and tiny yellow flowers that appear in summer. 'Bertram Anderson' is a variety with purple foliage and pink flowers in summer. All sedums prefer well-drained, moderately fertile soil. Height: 2–15cm; width: 30+cm. Sun to P.M. sun.

Sedum kamtschaticum
Russian Stonecrop

This sedum grows quickly and adapts to poor soils and dry periods, making it a good groundcover. Yellow flowers appear in summer. Prefers well-drained, moderately fertile soil. Displays succulent foliage and is clump-forming in habit. Height: 20–25cm; width: 30+cm. Sun to P.M. sun.

Sedum spurium
Two Row Stonecrop

A vigorously growing succulent with a mat-forming, creeping habit. Fleshy foliage ranges from bright green to deep burgundy. Produces pink, white or yellow flowers in summer. Tolerant of poor soils and dry periods. Prefers well-drained, moderately fertile soil. Height: 5–10cm; width: 45–60+cm. Sun to P.M. sun.

Sedum telephium
Stonecrop 'Matrona'

A very showy, clump-forming succulent with an upright habit. Purple-grey foliage displays orange-pink flowers in late summer to fall. Tolerant of poor soils and dry periods. Prefers well-drained, moderately fertile soil. Height: 40–45cm; width: 30cm. Sun to P.M. sun.

Sempervivum
Hen and Chicks

Drought-tolerant, evergreen, succulent rosettes form mats that are wonderful for edging or in rock gardens; interesting in containers. Available in different shades of grey, green and brown. Flowers may be purple, red, white or yellow and bloom in summer. Thrives in poor to moderately fertile, sharply drained, gritty soil—avoid winter wet. Height: 5–20cm; width: 15–30cm. Sun.

Sisyrinchium idahoense
Blue-Eyed Grass

These dainty clump-forming perennials resemble miniature irises and are very suitable for rock gardens. They self-seed freely. Produces dark-blue flowers with yellow eyes in summer. Prefers moist, well-drained soil. Avoid winter wet. Height; 10–20cm; width: 10–15cm. Sun.

Stachys byzantina
Lamb's Ears 'Silver Carpet'

This perennial is grown for its soft, silver-grey, woolly foliage and is a non-blooming variety. Excellent for edging, forming a thick spreading groundcover. Prefers fertile, well-drained soil but adapts well to dry sites. Height: 15–30cm; width: 45–60+cm. Sun to P.M. sun.

Thymus
Creeping Thyme

Thick, green, aromatic foliage forms a dense, spreading mat that will spill prettily over rocks. Displays pink flowers in early summer. Tolerates poor, dry sites once established. Thrives in well-drained, neutral to alkaline soil. Height: 2–5cm; width: 30–60+cm. Sun to P.M. sun.

Thymus pseudolanuginosus
Woolly Thyme

Thick, woolly, grey-green foliage forms a dense mat. Tolerates poor, dry sites once established. Plant between paving stones as it can withstand light foot traffic. Produces deep-pink flowers in late spring to early summer. Thrives in well-drained, neutral to alkaline soil. Height: 1–2cm; width: 30–45+cm. Sun to P.M. sun.

Thymus serpyllum
Mother of Thyme

Thick, woolly, grey-green, aromatic foliage forms a dense mat. Tolerates poor, dry sites once established. Plant in rockeries or along bed edges. Produces deep-pink flowers in late spring to early summer. Cut back after flowering to keep compact. Thrives in well-drained, neutral to alkaline soil. Height: 1–2cm; width: 30–45+cm. Sun to P.M. sun.

Veronica
Creeping Speedwell 'Waterperry Blue'

Creeping, mat-forming speedwells are wonderful groundcovers that are very pretty in bloom. Reintroduced recently, 'Waterperry Blue' is sure to rapidly regain popularity—it's perfect for rock gardens. Shiny green foliage highlights large, sky-blue flowers from late spring to early summer. Requires gritty, sharply drained, organic soil. Height: 10–15cm; width: 20–30cm. Sun to P.M. sun.

Veronica armena
Wooly Speedwell (Armenian Speedwell)

A wonderful clump-forming alpine plant for the rock garden or alpine scree bed. Rose-coloured flowers bloom in summer. Prefers sharply drained, organic, gritty soil. Height: 5–15cm; width: 30cm. Sun to P.M. sun.

Veronica oltensis
Creeping Speedwell (Thyme Leaf Speedwell)

Thrives in rock gardens or on rocky slopes. Mat-forming foliage and sub-shrubby habit supports azure-blue flowers from late spring to summer. Requires gritty, sharply drained, organic, alkaline soil. Height: 5–8cm; width: 15–20cm. Sun to P.M. sun.

Veronica thymoides
Creeping Speedwell

Used in rock gardens and rocky slopes, this plant forms a dense mat. Deep-blue to purple-blue flowers bloom in early summer atop grey-green foliage. Requires gritty, sharply drained, organic soil—avoid winter wet. Height: 2cm; width: 10–20cm. Sun to P.M. sun.

Veronicastrum virginicum
Culver's Root

Adds height to a mixed border and interesting texture with its whorls of leaves. Clump-forming and upright in habit. Spikes of white to pink or bluish-purple flowers in summer. Tolerates some dryness but prefers moist, fertile, organic soil. Height: 60–180cm; width: 45cm. Sun to P.M. sun.

Index

About the Author

Maggie Clayton was born and raised in Edmonton, Alberta and lived briefly in Australia and Singapore with her husband and two sons before settling in St. Albert, Alberta. Gardening has been a life-long passion for Maggie, but it became her career when she earned a diploma in Landscape Architectural Technology. Today, Maggie has a small practice where she applies her philosophy that gardening should be a pleasure and that there is an ideal landscape design for every gardener—regardless of his or her level of experience or environmental challenges.

About the Photographer

Akemi Matsubuchi was born in Montreal, Quebec and lived with her family on several continents before settling in St. Albert, Alberta. She attended Ryerson University where she received a Bachelor of Applied Arts in Still Photography. She has worked as a commercial and portrait photographer and photographed *Edmonton, Secrets of the City*. Akemi has been the primary photographer for 23 Hole's books, including the best-selling *Favorite* series and *Herbs and Edible Flowers*, for which she won an Alberta Book Illustration Award. Her work is regularly featured in the annual *Spring Gardening* magazine.

Acknowledgements

I would like to thank Shane Neufeld, former nursery manager at Hole's Greenhouse, whose knowledge of trees and shrubs was an invaluable resource for me. His enthusiasm for old garden standbys as well as for new introductions is infectious and always an inspiration to his staff and customers.

I am also grateful to all my clients and the gardeners who so generously shared their experiences, ideas and passions for many landscaping challenges and allowed us to photograph their gardens.

Thank you to the staff of Hole's Greenhouses and Gardens over the years, including but not limited to...

Christina McDonald
EDITOR

Carmen D. Hrynchuk
ASSISTANT EDITOR

Bruce Timothy Keith
PUBLICATION MANAGEMENT

Gregory Brown
DESIGN